WINGFIELD AT WAR

WINGFIELD
AT WAR

VOLUME 1 OF *THE BRITISH NAVY AT WAR AND PEACE*

MERVYN WINGFIELD

SERIES EDITOR: CAPTAIN PETER HORE

Published by
Whittles Publishing Ltd.,
Dunbeath,
Caithness, KW6 6EG,
Scotland, UK

www.whittlespublishing.com

Series editor: Captain P. G. Hore FRHistS CMIL RN rtd

ISBN 978-184995-064-0

Printed by
Ashford Colour Press Ltd, Gosport, Hampshire

CONTENTS

Captain Mervyn Wingfield DSO, DSC and bar, RN. 1911–2005

INTRODUCTION BY THE SERIES EDITOR

As a freelance obituarist for the Daily Telegraph I have written more than 500,000 words on over 500 men and women of the Royal Navy, Royal Marines, Merchant Navy and allied services including Special Forces personnel, yachtsmen, shipping magnates and others. An important national, daily broadsheet is a newspaper of record, and for an obituary to be published a very high degree of factual evidence is required. So, as well as enquiring about a man's or a woman's character, public achievements and private life, the obituarist is obliged to conduct much research and fact-checking.

There are three people who can be trusted with the amount and nature of information which needs to be sifted: they are the priest, the doctor, and   of course - the obituarist. Like the priest and the doctor, the obituarist must analyse much sensitive evidence, and must decide where the truth sits between the Official History, what the subject told the children, and what they and his or her friends remember – which can amount to many different things.

From time to time I have been trusted with unpublished memoirs or, as in this case, a full-blown autobiography. However, even these cannot be wholly relied upon because without recourse to official records and because the writing occurs many years after the event, the individual may easily make mistakes in dates and places, and in other matters.

Nevertheless, the individual may have been eyewitness to or protagonist in events which gave him or her a unique knowledge of what happened, and can recall details that historians are unaware of. In this series it is an honour to rescue this evidence from the grain of history and preserve it for this and future generations to read, mark and inwardly digest.

In this volume – as I will in future volumes - I have tried to keep the immediacy of the author's words, while making minor corrections only to the spelling and style. Also, by reference to official histories and especially in this case to Admiral Hezlet's *History of British Submarine Operations in the Second World War*, I have tried, by use of footnotes and endnotes, to give a framework to the story, to set it in its context, and to explain some of the names and places which the author assumed that the reader would know.

I am pleased that Mervyn Wingfield's memoirs should be the first in this series: *Wingfield at War* is told with a quiet humour, he is frank in his opinions and throughout his life he managed to shrug off its ups and downs. He has recorded events, like life in the pre-war Navy or hunting and then being hunted in his submarine off Penang, in a detail which deserves to be known more widely.

I am grateful to Richard Wingfield for providing his father's 1983 memoirs *A Sea-going Story*, from which he had produced an illustrated edition for the family in 2000, and for his help in sourcing further illustrations for the present edition, *Wingfield at War*. I am also grateful to Keith Whittles for his vision in agreeing to bring out this series of memoirs, and to Shelley Teasdale and Kerrie Moncur at Whittles Publishing for their unstinting work as editors and designers of this book.

PGH

FOREWORD

Captain Mervyn Wingfield was one of the last of his generation of submariners who made their reputation in World War II. Before the war he had served on the China station; in the war he commanded three submarines, *Umpire*, *Sturgeon* and *Taurus*, survived a collision in the North Sea, spent a winter in the Arctic, penetrated the Norwegian fjords submerged through a minefield, surfaced off St Nazaire in view of German guns to act as a navigation marker for the raiding force, fought cavalry in the northern Aegean, and later, off Penang, was the first to sink a Japanese submarine – and barely survived the subsequent, vicious counterattack after *Taurus* was severely damaged and became stuck in the mud at the bottom. Any one of these incidents would have merited a place for Wingfield in the history of naval warfare and the pantheon of submarine heroes. It is remarkable that one man should have been involved in so much action in so few years.

His naval career and mine barely overlapped, but I can empathise with some of Wingfield's deeds, in so far as the diesel-powered submarines in which I served were not so different to those in which he made his name years before, albeit that my boats were better equipped. So I can only admire his achievements, the risks that he took, and the manner in which he led his crew and was loved by them.

Many were burned out by the war, but in the post-war years Wingfield enjoyed a successful peacetime career where, finally, his personal qualities and his diplomacy were put to the test as a naval attaché.

I only regret that I never got to one of his famous, lively beef and Stilton lunches which he used to host at the Boat Show!

Wingfield belonged to one of the last of the generations of Anglo-Irish families who served the Crown and provided officers and men for the Army and the Navy, and his story gives some insights into his early days, especially with regard to being a young officer in the Royal Navy in the 1930s.

I commend his memoirs to the reader: Wingfield represents a passing generation, by any standard he was a hero, and he tells his life's story with modesty and humour.

Lord Boyce

PREFACE

These memoirs were written in 1982–83 primarily for the amusement of my family, and particularly my brother Tony in South Africa, who sadly died whilst the typescript was on its way to him. They make no claim to be a complete story of my life, but contain an account of those events which left a mark on my memory. As Voltaire said, 'Le secret d'ennuyer est celui de tout dire.'

After many years, there may be some mistakes in dates, places and names. If I have recaptured a little of the flavour of naval life during my time, I shall be quite satisfied.

Mervyn R.G. Wingfield

1

EARLY YEARS IN IRELAND (1911–21)

I f you are brought up in Southern Ireland in the first quarter of the 20th century and your parents are Low Church Protestants; if they are poor but aristocratic; if they disapprove of any form of drinking or gambling and dislike horses; if this is your youthful environment then it is likely that you will have a limited social life. Any potential friends are probably either too worldly or too common or, worst of all, Catholics.

I was brought up to look on Catholics as beyond the pale (to use an old Irish expression meaning beyond the palings which surrounded the Protestant fortresses). High Church Protestants were little better and were known as 'Anglo Cats'. Encouraged as I was to look on the native population as subhuman, I have some sympathy with those children in Ulster who are educated in fiercely sectarian schools.

Thus in Greystone, Co. Wicklow, where I spent my first ten years (I was born on 16 January 1911), we led a fairly isolated life. I had, it is true, three elder sisters and two elder brothers, which meant a certain amount of family life, but also contributed to the genteel poverty in which we lived. Amazingly, all of this large family went to public schools, or the girls' equivalent, except perhaps the third daughter, Rosalie. She was judged to be delicate and was educated largely by governesses. (Now, sixty-odd years later, she enjoys robust health!)

Mention of governesses brings me to what is certainly my first recollection. It must have been about 1914 when the current governess, or nurse in my case, who was German, taught me the nursery rhyme:

This is the church, this is the steeple,
Open the doors and see all the people.
This is the Parson going upstairs,
And this is the Parson saying his prayers.

I can still recite this in a rough version of German.

We had an Aunt Zinnie who was married to a German army officer stationed, I seem to remember, in Frankfurt am Main. Each Christmas she sent us a big box of cakes, sweets and biscuits. I remember the welcome arrival of these goodies, including my particular favourite, marzipan piglets. I can taste them to this day!

The outbreak of war passed me by, but I have a picture in my mind of lifeboats full of ragged people rowing into harbour. I can't be sure they were survivors of the ocean liner *Lusitania* arriving in Kinsale but it seems quite likely.[1] On the other hand, I may be thinking of one of the dramatic pictures in the *Illustrated London News*. The sinking of the Dublin–Liverpool mailboat *Leinster* also sticks in my mind.[2] Some relation was on board, but whether she survived or was a U-boat victim, I do not know. I would like to think that these early events impressed me with the effectiveness of undersea warfare and thus influenced my later life, but I think that would be going too far.

I have a very clear picture of my eldest brother, Dick, in uniform and wearing a sword, presumably just before he left to join the Field Artillery in Mesopotamia where, alas, he was very soon killed. When the War Office telegram arrived my mother and sisters were deeply affected but at the age of six I was less involved. One of the sisters said, 'Why aren't you crying? Don't you realise Dick has been killed?'

Impressed as I evidently was with uniforms, there is one event which I can date exactly: the Easter Rebellion of 1916, when Sinn Feiners murdered a score of British officers in their beds. My father, on leave from the Western Front, put on his uniform (and sword of course) and announced that he was going up to Dublin to help. Apparently he did not get much of a welcome at Dublin Castle, as he returned home in time for tea. Even to my five-year-old eyes he appeared crestfallen.

I can remember some happy days in that period but I suffered from being so obviously unloved and unwanted. Some years later I ventured to remark somewhat precociously that birth control seemed a good idea. My mother, in a burst of untypical frankness, slapped me down with 'You shouldn't say too much about that. If birth control had been invented in 1910 you wouldn't be here.'

My elders seemed much concerned with keeping me in my place. They made it clear that I was stupid and useless. Every idea of mine was derided and my activities ridiculed. Small wonder that I grew up totally lacking in confidence and successful at nothing. Not until late in my school years did I make my first breakthrough.

Religion played a large part in my life at this time. Apart from a lot of churchgoing, in summer we had to attend children's services on the beach and there was much evangelistic pressure. My mother never gave up her efforts to make me join religious organisations. Later on I was constantly harried by the Officers' Christian Union, with which she had some connection, but I found myself repelled by the fervency of their advocates. My mother looked on me as a brand to be plucked from the burning and a potential recruit to evangelism. She did not seem much interested in me as a person.

A few more childhood memories come back to me. My first ride in a motor car was a great experience. The car was an open Overland and we went off in it for a picnic. I am pretty sure the owner was called Miss Frost and I know she wore a motoring veil. Another car I once rode in belonged to 'The Aunts', who lived in Killiney. They were in fact the great-aunts and were pretty well off. Their car was a Daimler of the type which rose in steps from a low bonnet. (Queen Alexandra was in one of these when I saw her near Sandringham in about 1923.) I should think its year was about 1910. The former coachman was chauffeur and only he had the trick of starting it. This saved it from requisitioning by the Sinn Feiners when they raided the house one day, I believe. The Aunts paid most of our school fees, otherwise we could not possibly have gone to Marlborough (both brothers), Sherborne, Cheltenham and Dartmouth.

Ireland had a fairly easy time in the First War. There was no rationing and we seemed to have plenty of lamb (never beef), sugar and butter. There were, however, strict regulations for people living on the coast. These were broken on 11 November 1918 when we celebrated the Armistice Day with a firework display. My father had a Very pistol from which he fired quantities of rockets of all colours into the air. A policeman called next day to say that we had caused much trouble to ships at sea who thought the rockets came from a ship in distress.[3]

We had an interesting next door neighbour at this time, the rebel leader de Valera. One day the *Daily Mail* had a headline 'Where is de Valera?' He had apparently been allowed to escape from Mountjoy Prison where he was an embarrassment to the British. We knew where he was: just across the garden fence digging his potatoes!

It must have been 1920 when the battleships *Queen Elizabeth* and *Barham* visited Dublin Bay. I was allowed to join the throng of visitors and was lucky enough to be invited to tea in the wardroom of the *Queen Elizabeth*. Never had I seen such delicious iced cakes or such succulent ice creams. There and then I made the resolve to join the Navy at all costs.

It was about this time that some relation took Rosalie and me out in his yacht *Ethne*. In retrospect I think it was of the class known as Dublin Bay 24-footers. I thoroughly enjoyed the lively motion and explored the forepeak where there was the smell, romantic to me, of Stockholm tar and canvas. I was deeply hurt to be greeted with jeers and accusations of being seasick. Not then or ever after have I suffered from this complaint. There is nothing discreditable in succumbing to this, it is just that you are born with it.

In 1920 or 1921 my father resumed his clerical career. After many years in the Artillery he took Holy Orders in about 1913, becoming curate of Wigan. He was not there long before being recalled to the army, where he served as a combatant officer in Gallipoli and the Western Front and received the DSO (the miniature DSO which I wear was his).

The parish to which he was appointed was Broome, near Bungay, Suffolk. This was like a foreign country to us and we could hardly understand the natives. We had a large but unmodernised rectory and a fine garden with an Upper and Lower Lake (actually small muddy ponds).

[Above left] Mervyn's father William Edward Wingfield at RMA Woolwich in 1890 before joining the Royal Horse Artillery and [Above right] as Lt Col (Rev) in the Royal Field Artillery around 1920

Mervyn's mother Elizabeth Trench

In spite of adding the neighbouring parish of Thwaite to Broome, thus increasing his income, my father was earning only the pay of a rural clergyman. Nevertheless, we had a gardener/handyman called Cunningham, who had been my father's batman during the war. He spoke with a delightful Irish accent and could turn his hand to anything. His duties included pumping water from the well up to the tank in the attic and emptying the outside earth closet.

We had no car until after we had been at Broome for several years, but I seem to remember my father riding an early type of light motorcycle. My mother had a pony trap which was pulled by a donkey, very, very slowly.

Every morning after breakfast we had Family Prayers which was attended by all the children at home and the staff, i.e. Cunningham, Mrs Savage the cook, and a maid called Annie who was slightly soft in the head. For some years there was also Grandma Wingfield, a formidable character who had been through the Indian Mutiny in 1857. She endeared herself to me by insisting on my being allowed a glass of her Burgundy on my tenth birthday, much to my mother's displeasure. I still find Burgundy my favourite wine.

On Sundays we all walked to church. Even when we had a car this was never used on Sundays, a relic of the custom of giving the horses a day of rest. The congregation was quite good, considering how far the church was from the village, and my father preached rousing sermons. He also organised the villagers into acting plays written by himself. One I remember was called *The Baluch Hero* with the cast in splendid Indian costumes. It was an achievement to get stolid Suffolk yokels on to the stage but they seemed to enjoy it. My father was musically inclined and had what he called a one-man band consisting of a banjo with a mouth organ attached, cymbals on his knees which he banged together, also a triangle and a drum which he beat with a foot pedal. Sometimes he would play a portable harmonium at open-air services.

His great hobby was mountain climbing and every year he would go off to Switzerland for two or three weeks. It was on one of these holidays in 1926 that he was taken ill and died at the early age of sixty. He suffered a heart attack climbing the Matterhorn and was buried at Zermatt.

My father was an excellent raconteur and like many an Irishman he was reluctant to spoil a good story by too pedantic an adherence to the truth. His accounts of the battles of the Boer War entranced me and it was only some years later that I realised that he had been in India at the time and had never set foot in South Africa.

2

SCHOOL DAYS (1922–28)

I never went to a proper prep school, but received some elementary education at a little private day school near Broome, to which I cycled. The weather was often wet and cold but off I went every day, rain or shine. It was, I suppose, in 1922 that I was sent to Aunt Bessie (Pike) in Bedford with whom I lived in term time, while attending, for one term, Rushmoor School. This was a brutal establishment. The regular punishment was beating on the hands with a billiard cue. This sometimes made holding a pen difficult. The old traditions of Rushmoor apparently continued long afterwards, as in 1982 I read in a newspaper that the headmaster had been convicted of physical assault on a pupil.

Aunt Bessie (actually a sister of my Uncle Crosbie Trench's wife) was an impoverished widow of an army officer of modest rank who died young. He was never mentioned and it is possible that he 'drank'. However, he fathered three remarkable sons, all of whom were educated at Bedford School (not to be confused with Bedford Modern School). Roy, the eldest, won scholarships and prizes of all kinds. He became an astronomer and was widely tipped to be the Astronomer Royal at a ridiculously early age. Sadly he died in his thirties of 'brain-fever' brought on, I was told, by excessive mental exertion. Bill, the second son, joined the Royal Artillery and finished up with the re-sounding title of Vice Chief of the Imperial General Staff.[4] He lives a few miles away from us now and I occasionally have the pleasure of meeting him.

Geoff, the third son, was the one I saw most of as he was at Bedford School when I was staying with his mother. He joined the RAF and became a brilliant pilot. His rise was rapid and by 1939 he was a Group Captain. I think he had only a short period combat flying in night fighters, but as they were the first fighter aircraft to have radar he had little difficulty in knocking down a good score of enemy bombers and collecting a quick DSO and DFC. He finished his career as Marshal of the Royal Air Force, Sir Thomas Geoffrey Pike, KCB, DSO, DFC, etc. etc., Chief of the Air Staff.[5]

In 1923 Aunt Bessie moved to a nearby village called Lidlington and I became the lowest of the low at Bedford School. Not a boarder, not a day-boy, but a train-boy. We were universally despised because we arrived late and left early and took no part in games. Rugger was (and still is) of great importance at Bedford. I can still remember that the captain of the 1st XV was called Starkey – a hero to us all. I was nominally in Mr Simmond's house but saw little of him or it. Looming large in my life were two masters, Mr Sewell (the Nipper) and Mr Mumford. The former taught Latin and was a great believer in the educational value of three or four cuts of the cane. This punishment was administered at the end of the period in the presence of another master acting as 'referee'. Many was the time I was sent to present Mr Sewell's compliments to Mr Mumford and could he spare a few minutes to act in this capacity.

Scholastically I was backward in every subject, being particularly bad at Latin. Once Mr Sewell sent a letter which I had to deliver to my guardian. I remember its wording:

> MRG Wingfield. This boy is idle, untidy and inattentive. If he does not improve it will not be possible for him to remain at this school. (Signed) RJ Sewell

What with discouragement at home and at school, it was with little confidence that I took the entry examination for the Royal Navy College, Dartmouth in December 1923.

First came the interview, but not quite first. Before anything else, Messrs Gieves' representative measured every candidate for his uniform. Obviously half his work was wasted, but it ensured that every one of the fifty-two successful candidates would order his cadet's outfit from Gieves. This usually started a lifetime association with this splendid firm. Long credit was the rule and almost every officer had a monthly allotment of a few pounds to Gieves.

Later on I heard a story which amused me. A certain extravagant young officer received a letter from Gieves requesting him to pay off a little of his large account. 'Dear Sir', he wrote. 'I must explain to you my system of paying bills. Each month I put all the accounts I have received in a top hat, shake them up and pull out one, which I pay. If I receive any further communications like the one which I have just received from you, I shall not even put your bill in the hat.'

The interview, in the palatial surroundings of Burlington House, went quite well. There was the usual row of admirals and all the usual questions, even the one about which were our three most famous admirals. Traditionally one was supposed to reply 'Rodney, Nelson, and I didn't quite catch your name, Sir', but I added Jellicoe, which went down quite well, although the Beatty–Jellicoe dispute about Jutland was at its height just then.[6] I was also asked if I had any relatives in the Navy. 'Yes,' I replied, 'I have a brother-in-law who is a lieutenant in submarines.' Long pause. 'Would that be your sister's husband?' 'Yes Sir.' I resisted the temptation to add 'not being married myself'. Shortly afterwards I was informed that I had passed the interview. So far so good, but there was still the written exam, a daunting prospect. I found the papers, except for English and History, somewhat beyond me, particularly the Latin which I could make no sense of. A week or two later, back at Broome Rectory, I received a letter to say that I had failed.

This threw me into the depths of depression and confirmed my belief, apparently shared by my family, that I was a failure at everything. However, to give my father credit, he somehow discovered that there was a back door into Dartmouth via the Nautical College, Pangbourne, Berkshire. So it was that in January 1924 I put on the uniform of a cadet, Royal Naval Reserve.

PANGBOURNE COLLEGE (1924–25)

The Nautical College in those days had a strong sailing ship tradition. It was founded in 1920 by the shipowners Devitt and Moore, who were among the last to trade in square-riggers. All their ships carried a good contingent of cadets or apprentices, who of course paid a premium for their training. This enabled the company to take on the minimum of paid seamen and to make large profits even at the very end of the sailing ship era. When they finally ceased trading the cadets were put ashore and formed the nucleus of the Nautical College. The idea was to prepare boys for the Merchant Service on the same lines as the long-established training ships *Worcester* and *Conway*.

Navigation and seamanship were taken seriously. Most of the instructors were ex-sailing ship men, and to this day I can remember the names of the innumerable wires, ropes, sheets, tacks, guys and stays of a three-masted barque.

We slept in hammocks, which enabled the management to pack a dozen cadets into a room which would have held four bodies in an ordinary school. We drilled and marched and did 'field-work'. If today you admire the smooth turf of the college cricket field, bear in mind that the ground was cleared and levelled by generations of bygone cadets in their recreation time. Cheap labour, indeed.

I was reasonably happy at Pangbourne but made no mark in work or sport. Both here and later at Dartmouth, only the good players were given any sports instruction. The duffers like me fielded listlessly at longstop or trotted after the forwards, seldom touching the ball and hating every minute of it. Nobody ever told me that the secret of every ball game is to keep your eye on the ball and watch it right on to the bat, racket or stick. Not until I became a moderate golfer did this truth dawn on me. By then it was too late. I never did learn to catch a cricket ball. I remember pleasant afternoons on the Thames in the college boats and picnics in the woods. The smell of wood smoke still makes me think of frying sausages over an open fire.

After three terms at Pangbourne I was sent to the Royal Naval College, Dartmouth, to sit the end-of-term exams with the Duncan term which I would have joined if I had passed originally. Fortunately there was no Latin and the result was a pass by the narrowest of margins. I and a fellow Pangbourne cadet were 47th and 49th respectively out of 50 and were accepted as Cadets RN. We joined the college in January 1925.

DARTMOUTH COLLEGE (1925–28)

The Royal Naval College, Dartmouth, is an imposing building, over-shadowing the harbour and town. The college had its origins in the old three-decker *Britannia* which lay in the Dart for thirty or forty years, and many of the old traditions persisted. One of the most curious was the segregation of cadets in terms. These were groups of about fifty cadets, all exactly the same age, who had no contact with members of other terms. To speak to a senior would be cheek or 'guff' as it was called; to speak to a junior was beneath one's dignity. I was in the Duncan term, not a distinguished one, but having, even today, some remains of our fierce loyalty to its memory, as witness our term reunions which persisted up to the 55th anniversary of our joining the college. I think the term system was a bad one and I am glad to know that it was replaced by a house system more in line with other public schools. (Dartmouth was a public school, as were Bedford and Pangbourne. As I tell my friends, not many people have been to three!)

Each term had A, B and C classes in each subject. I was mostly in the Cs. At least this resulted in my not having to learn calculus! Seamanship, which consisted largely of knots, splices, bends and hitches, I found easier, although there was, it seemed to me, excessive emphasis on learning the archaic names of out-of-date equipment. We did not learn geography at all as it was deemed unnecessary for young officers who would soon be seeing the world at first hand. Latin, thank goodness, was also out, but naval history loomed large. I think it was rather badly taught. None of our naval heroes could have been quite as perfect as they were depicted in our history books. (Looking back, it occurs to me that there was a nice little fiddle going on among the masters. Many of them had written books on their special subjects which we had to buy new each term. Over the years this must have produced a good income.)

Another subject given some importance was engineering. There were extensive workshops down on the river with a large staff of pensioner Engine Room Artificers and Stoker Petty Officers. I have always believed that it is best for deck officers to leave engineering matters to the engineers. Nothing but resentment is caused by a captain who pretends to a knowledge of mechanical matters and presumes to advise his chief engineer. However, I suppose the long hours we spent on wood and metal working, and studying the innards of ships' machinery, may have contributed to what little skill I have in DIY.

My final position in the term when we passed out in March 1928 was 37th. It is some consolation to me that the top cadet of the term did not achieve promotion to commander and was last heard of writing technical handbooks for the Torpedo School. Similarly, the second, who was a descendant of generations of admirals, was to run a profitable chain of launderettes. The only one of the Duncan term to make the rank of admiral was Frewen.[7] He passed out 17th. We called him 'Ikey' Frewen. Despite a Jewish appearance he was said not to have an ounce of Jewish blood in him. His family, who lived in some style at Brede Place in Sussex, had been prominent in late Victorian and Edwardian society. It would have been a source of astonishment to me at the time, and no doubt to all who knew me then, that second in rank to Admiral Frewen on the conclusion of the naval careers of all the Duncan term was a certain Captain Mervyn R. G. Wingfield.

There was considerable emphasis on sport – cricket, rugby, hockey (a little), rowing and sailing. Only the stars were ever given instruction but each of us had to do a 'log' every afternoon except Sunday. This meant playing an organised game – squash counted as half a log and you had to do something else like going for a run to make up a full log. If the weather was too bad 'Optional Landing' was piped (a relic of *Britannia*) and most of us trooped to the canteen, i.e. tuck-shop. I remember the best value for size was a Penny Sponge. Washed down with Cherry Ciderette it was pure heaven. But for the rich boys (and there were quite a few with allowances far above the official one shilling a week), the 'in' dish was banana, Devonshire cream and brown sugar. All this mashed up into a delicious goo. I still love it.

In view of my later interest in yachting it may seem surprising that sailing, as practised at the college, gave me an aversion to this form of recreation which lasted for twenty years. Service cutters, in which we were supposed to be taught how to sail, were open boats with two masts, one dipping big sail and one gunter. They had six thwarts and were rowed by twelve oarsmen. They had no drop keel and were virtually incapable of going to windward. The usual routine was for a class of cadets under a pensioner chief petty officer to embark at Sandquay. We then shipped the masts, hoisted sails and sailed off downwind. If we had to gybe or wear, it was necessary to dip the yard of the mainsail round the mast and reset it on the lee side.

By now we would be near the harbour mouth so the order was given to lower sails and masts and take to the oars. The tide was now against us as well as the wind. We made little progress. At about 5 p.m. a steam launch would arrive and tow us back to our mooring. It was probably raining. A miserable afternoon, enough to cure anyone of a taste for yachting. To be fair, there were some other boats which we used. I remember blueboats, two-oared skiffs, and I think some antique gaff-rigged 20-footers. But the instructors did not know anything about yacht sailing.

The trouble was that in the 1920s sailing had only just ceased to be normal for work-boats and it had not yet become a sport. I was to see the rise of naval sailing to its peak in the late 1940s and 1950s, when members of the Royal Naval Sailing Association won many of the major prizes. One must admit that it was mostly due to one man, Captain John Illingworth, yacht racing champion, yacht designer and a friend.[8] In Fleet Sailing Regattas in later years the average standard of skill was very low. The one or two officers who had yachting experience and knew how to set and trim sails cleaned up all the prizes with no difficulty.

Another enjoyable activity on Sunday afternoons was to walk to a farmhouse a few miles away and have tea. This was no affair of lacy cucumber sandwiches and seed cake. Scrambled eggs to start with, quantities of bread and strawberry jam lavishly coated with Devonshire cream and finally fruit cake in segments of at least 25 degrees. Next, a packet of Kensitas would be furtively produced and we would all have a puff of these disgusting cigarettes. Tea was 2s. 6d.

When the farmer's wife asked us if we would like a small glass of home-brewed cider to finish off with, we accepted with glee. Anyone who has been in the West Country will know that farmhouse cider is powerful tackle. The college would have put that farm out of bounds had they known. Scrumpy is curious stuff. As one who has tried most of the world's popular beverages, I can say that it affects one's legs before one's brain. You are happily sitting on your bar stool enjoying your pint of scrumpy and feeling reasonably sober. When you get up, you fall down! However, we usually giggled our way back in time for evensong at the chapel.

The great thing about Dartmouth was to keep one occupied all the time. A bell rang at 7.00 a.m. and we all got up, shed our pyjamas and went through the cold plunge. Every dormitory, which housed a whole term, had a shallow bath about 12 feet by 12 feet full of cold water into which we dived, if we were dashing, or crept reluctantly if we were not. I think this was designed to curb our sensual desires. Another bell rang and we went down to breakfast. I must say the food at Dartmouth was good. We paid fees but the whole establishment ran at an enormous loss. There were more employees than cadets. Once I told my mother that we had chicken and butter and Devonshire cream, to which she replied that she was sorry that I did not feed as well in the holidays as at school. Bugle calls to wake us up, bells to put us on our knees for prayers at bedtime, bells for lights-out, every minute was regulated. Moving about the college we had to double (i.e. run) all the time until we were senior termers. No hands allowed in pockets (no trouser pockets for juniors!), certain paths were reserved for cadet captains, special methods of marching at divisions, the whole place was a maze of protocol.

And then there was the tick system. For minor offences such as talking after lights-out, having untidily folded clothes or failing to complete a 'log', a cadet captain could award a 'tick'. If you scored three of these you were called from your bed and given three cuts of the cane by the cadet captain. I have never heard of this system in any other school but I suppose it was effective in its way.

SOME PERSONALITIES AND THE
GREAT DIRTY POSTCARD SCANDAL

When I joined, the captain of the college, an Olympian figure, was Sir Herbert Meade-Featherstonehaugh. I don't think I ever saw him as I kept a low profile during my first term. I was reminded of him when I visited Uppark recently.[9] This was his family home and here in his ancestors' day there was a housemaid called Emma. She was a great success with the squire and his foxhunting friends and when she danced on the dining room table in a version of the seven veils, the applause was terrific. Sadly she became pregnant at the age of sixteen and had to be sacked. Thus she started on a road which took her to the glittering world of Naples as the wife of our ambassador and the mistress of Lord Nelson. She was Emma Hamilton, the Divine Lady.

Captain Martin Dunbar-Nasmith VC was the next captain. A submarine hero of World War II, he was decorated for an astonishing patrol in the submarine *E.11*. He penetrated the Dardanelles and for weeks wreaked havoc in the Sea of Marmara. I believe he even had a battle once with Turkish horse cavalry. (See Chapter 12 for my encounter with Bulgarian cavalry) He was said to be terrified of sex and to have ordered the climbing ropes to be removed from the gymnasium in case the cadets got pleasurable sensations sliding down them.

In my 10th term I was promoted to cadet captain. This was a moment of total glory. It was the first success of any kind I had achieved in my life. (A cadet captain is the equivalent of an under-officer at Sandhurst or a public school prefect.) My family received the news with something less than acclamation. 'Oh yes,' said my mother. 'What is a cadet captain? Is it good?' This was a little disappointing but the stripe on my arm was a constant joy and I started off happily in charge of the 9th term.

When Cadet Morris, one of my term mates, was put under arrest for selling dirty postcards to junior terms, the college rocked. It appeared that he had answered an advertisement in the back pages of the *Tatler* for art studies of famous actresses. Many were of June, a famous pin-up of the day, who was not averse to posing in a diaphanous negligee.

15

She had a face like an angel and married and divorced the 2nd Lord Inverclyde.

Several cadet captains (but not me) were involved in the postcard traffic and they were all in trouble. Incidentally, the postcards themselves would not cause a single eyebrow to be raised today, but I suppose they were faintly titillating. The captain of the college decided he must take the sternest action to stamp out this evil and all the cadet captains involved were disrated to cadet. For Morris things were more serious. He was sentenced to twelve cuts of the cane, these to be Official Cuts and entered into his record.

Then followed an astonishing scene which might have come straight out of Captain Marryat's novels. The entire Duncan term was marched to the gymnasium and fallen in, in single ranks, against the wall bars. In the centre was a box-horse with a group round it including the captain, commander, surgeon lieutenant and two physical training instructors. Soon the unfortunate Morris was marched in and the Warrant for Punishment read. (In this case it had been approved by the commander-in-chief, Plymouth.) The captain then asked the surgeon lieutenant if the prisoner was fit to receive punishment. 'Fit for punishment, Sir,' replied the doctor. 'Carry on then, chief petty officer,' said the captain.

The two physical training instructors (one of them left-handed) flexed their muscles, made a few practice swings and then in slow time proceeded to administer twelve resounding cuts. Morris, who was bent over the box-horse, made scarcely a sound but three of his fellow cadets fainted slap on the floor with dramatic effect. Even at the time, it seemed to me that what I was watching was an 18th-century naval flogging.

The punishment complete, the officers departed and Morris was led to the sickbay to have his wounds dressed. These were quite spectacular when he showed them to us later in the dormitory. As they healed they turned all the colours of the rainbow.

On the day after the flogging of Morris, I was summoned to the captain's office. 'Wingfield,' said Captain Dunbar-Nasmith, 'I find myself in an invidious position. I have had to disrate three cadet captains and one term cadet captain, for whom I have to find replacements. I have decided that I must promote you to term cadet captain. That is all.'

Although I didn't know what 'invidious' meant, it sounded like making the best of unsatisfactory alternatives, which was scarcely complimentary. However, I was delighted and hurried away to have a star sewn on my arm. It's an ill wind …

In those days the officers of the Fleet were drawn from the upper or upper-middle class, many of them sons of service families, some with long naval traditions, and also from the aristocracy, including a sprinkling of princes, some foreign. In the Duncan term we had an Irish baronet and a viscount, the latter a descendant of Nelson's brother. He was also Duke of Bronte, I think. 'Hons' were plentiful. The story was that Prince George, who was a little senior to me, was kept very short of pocket money. He wrote to his mother, Queen Mary, asking for a couple of pounds. She replied with a stern refusal. The Prince answered, 'Dear Mother, I am sorry you couldn't spare me a little extra pocket money, but all is well as I sold your letter to another cadet for £5.' Some years later Prince George, by now a lieutenant, incurred a rather large bill at a well-known house of doubtful repute in Hong Kong. The proprietress, by name Ethel Morrison, sent her 'shroff' (debt collector) to the Prince several times to collect the money but with no success. Wishing to avoid any scandal she decided to pass the buck, and so dropped the chit signed 'George P' in the collection bag at the Cathedral. 'Let the Dean worry about that,' she said.

Another cadet a few terms senior to me achieved fame in the thirties as the 'Officer in the Tower'. Baillie-Stewart was removed from the college after some minor scandal and entered Sandhurst.[10] He was commissioned in the Seaforth Highlanders, then serving in Aldershot. He spent all his leaves in Germany and became a fervent supporter of Hitler. He eventually started doing some amateur spying for the Nazis but was soon arrested and imprisoned in the Tower of London. There he took his daily exercise in the moat dressed in full uniform and kilt, to the delight of hordes of press photographers.

At the passing-out parade from Dartmouth we usually had some distinguished personage to take the salute and make a speech. One I remember was Admiral of the Fleet Sir Osmond de Beauvoir Brock. He was very elderly (all admirals were to our eyes) and he said we might be interested in the experience of a relative of his. When he was about ten years old his great-uncle, in his eighties, had told him in great detail the story of a battle between the frigates *Chesapeake* and *Shannon*. Lieutenant Brock had been first lieutenant of the *Shannon*, which was the winner of the duel. It took place just outside Boston, Massachusetts, on 1 June 1813 and was watched by a spectator fleet of local yachts. The casualties on both sides were enormous but *Chesapeake* was the first to strike her colours. A famous victory, but one of the very few we had in the War of 1812. It is nice to have heard about it, albeit at second hand.

Two other cadets left the college prematurely. One was expelled after a farmer's daughter at Stoke Fleming became pregnant. He joined the army and commanded a company of the Chindits in Burma. Another was removed on scholastic grounds, joined a Guards regiment and was killed at El Alamein.

3

I JOIN THE FLEET (1928–30)

Battleship HMS Benbow

March 1928 saw five apprehensive cadets waiting at the Fleet Landing at Sheerness to join their first ship. HMS *Benbow*, built about 1912, was a coal-burning battleship of the *Iron Duke* class mounting ten 13.5-inch guns in five turrets. It was wet and cold as we huddled in the picket boat. The great moment had arrived; we mounted the gangway, saluted the quarterdeck (a relic of the days when it held a crucifix) and said our piece: 'Come aboard to join, Sir'. The welcome we received was not warm.

'They seem a scruffy lot', said Lieutenant Commander Vale. 'Sub, they've got their Burberry collars turned up. Take them down to the

HMS Benbow *coaling, Oban 1928*

Coaling team, HMS Benbow;
Wingfield standing far right

bathroom and give them three cuts each to teach them how officers dress.' 'Porky' Vale was the Snotties Nurse, or in plain language, the officer in charge of midshipmen's instruction and discipline. With hindsight I am fairly sure he was half-drunk – he often was.

Our first impressions were of pride. Here was a battleship gunroom living up to all the stories we had read of the great days of the Grand Fleet. Three cuts were nothing after our years at Dartmouth.

The gunroom in this class of battleship was three decks down and had no portholes. Air was blown in through louvres, each of which had a blue uniform sock over its end to catch the coal dust. It was grossly overcrowded and almost Hogarthian in its squalor. At one end lounged the sub-lieutenant and the five senior midshipmen. They all smoked incessantly, drank quantities of gin and had plenty of money to spend ashore. One was a Siamese prince named Abhakara Karajitphol, but always called Sam. I asked him once if he was related to Ned, a well-known racing driver. He said he was a half-brother. 'My father has many wives.' Poor Ned was killed when he collided with a lamppost in Piccadilly at high speed in the early hours.

Another of the senior mids was Brocklebank. His father was a shipping tycoon and I remember him for the fact that he was quite the most dissolute of his group.

Benbow was the flagship of the 3rd Battle Squadron, whose function was boys' training. Each ship carried a couple of hundred seventeen-year-old boy seamen fresh from their training establishment. *Iron Duke* (Jellicoe's flagship at Jutland), *Marlborough* and *Emperor of India* made up the squadron. My aforementioned brother-in-law, Hugh Mundy, was a lieutenant in *Emperor of India*. He had been in submarines and had taken me out in his H-boat for a day trip while I was at Pangbourne, which was a great thrill and must have sown a seed.

'Coaling ship' was a tremendous operation which took place every six weeks. Everyone except the band, the captain and the officer of the watch took part and it was on a competitive basis between the four ships.

First the ship would be prepared for coaling. All living quarters, pantries and so on were sealed up with newspaper pasted over the cracks. The screen derricks would be rigged and adjusted to plumb the collier's holds. The whole ship's company including the officers would (to use the curious naval phrase) 'clean into coaling rig'. Some good advice was received by us new boys before the first coal ship: 'Cover your face, ears and neck with grease, preferably cocoa butter, before coaling starts. This is the only way to get rid of the coal dust when you finish.'

Then the collier, which I remember was called *Frances Duncan*, came alongside. Each of her four holds was alongside one of our derricks. The method was simple. Each hold contained six gangs of four men who filled the coal bags, usually six or eight, but occasionally nine or ten if they shovelled really hard. A senior midshipman stood on top of the central pile of coal and caught the hook of the derrick purchase. Then with a flying leap he delivered the hook to the gang who had a hoist of bags ready with wire strops through the steel rings on the bags. Immediately the derrick operator hoisted away at full speed and the wildly swinging hoist was deposited on the battleship's deck. All this was great fun, but slightly dangerous. There were always a few injuries, but I only saw one boy sailor killed. He unfortunately got between the swinging hoist and a bulkhead.

Once on deck the bags were quickly loaded on to trolleys and pushed to the manholes, where they were upturned and emptied. Twenty feet below in the dimly lit bunkers, the stokers performed the unpleasant task of trimming the coal. There was no ventilation so the atmosphere can be imagined.

During coaling the Royal Marine Band played on top of X-turret. Small numeral flags at the yardarm showed the number of tons loaded in the last hour and tin 'Fannies' of lime juice laced with rum were sent down to us in the collier's hold. Competition between ships was intense. My recollection is that we were usually champions (it would be!) with about 340 tons per hour. This was nothing like the record of the Grant Fleet ships of ten years before. I heard that *Iron Duke* used to reach 420 tons per hour, but then she was fully commissioned with a proper crew, not a boys' training ship.

Coaling finished with perhaps 2,000 tons aboard and the problem then was to clean oneself and then the ship. We boasted that the coal-burning ships were much cleaner than the oil-fired ones because they washed the whole ship all over every few weeks. If you had taken the precaution of putting on grease, the coal washed off fairly easily under a hot shower. Then one's filthy coaling rig was put away in newspaper in one's chest with some relief until next required.

An old tradition and a great feature of a midshipman's life was a form of institutionalised bullying called Gunroom Evolutions. These were performed by the junior mids for the amusement of the sub-lieutenant and senior mids. At the shout of 'Dogs of War – Out Mr X', the juniors forcibly removed the selected mid who, of course, fought bitterly. Where the gunroom had a porthole, he would often be pushed through it to swim to the gangway. 'Breadcrumbs' meant all the juniors must stop their ears. Cock-fighting – one mid on another's back, Pyramids when four storeys of bodies on hands and knees became a flattened heap on the order of 'Down!', Priest of the Parish – too complicated to explain, and the popular 'Are you there, Moriarty?' played by two blindfolded mids armed with rolled up copies of the *Illustrated London News*, all these were on the programme after dinner.

I should explain that we all dressed for dinner every night, except on Sundays and when at sea. We wore boiled shirts, stiff collars and the sort of pageboy coat called a round jacket. These were apt to suffer some damage as a result of Evolutions, as did the gunroom furniture. I do not remember resenting any of this; in fact I think we were rather proud to be in *Benbow*, which had the reputation for being a tough ship.

We made three cruises a year in the training squadron calling at places like Torbay, Milford Haven, Firth of Clyde, Scapa Flow and lastly

Invergordon. There we would join the rest of the Atlantic Fleet for a few weeks of gunnery practice and rest and recreation. The firing of the 13.5-inch guns was quite an event as economy was running rife in 1929 and very few full calibre shells were available. Nevertheless, I was in the spotting top, high on the foremast, when we fired a broadside of all ten 13.5s at once. The noise was unbelievable, the whole ship shook and the mast whipped violently.

I have a vivid memory of one calm evening at Invergordon with the loch full of ships: two squadrons of battleships, three battle cruisers, eight or more cruisers and destroyers and smaller ships by the score. At 9 p.m. the Preparative flag was hauled down in the flagship *Nelson*. Immediately the buglers in every ship sounded the Still followed by the haunting and long-drawn notes of Sunset. The sound of the bugles over the still waters and echoing from the mountains was very moving and somehow made one immensely proud to be part of the Royal Navy.

I rather blotted my copybook on this cruise by sinking a whaler. The commander required some more sand for scrubbing decks, a daily chore which, with polishing brass work, took up the early hours of every day. I was told to take the whaler, under sail of course as it had been for Admiral Benbow himself, to Nigg at the entrance to the loch where the seashore provided the best quality of scrubbing sand. We beached the boat and turned to with a will, shovelling in the sand. I had no idea how much she would carry, but when she was about half full I called a halt. The tide rose, but the whaler did not. Soon water covered boat and cargo and I was forced to wait for another tide to reduce the load of sand by half. I was the object of some derision, to put it mildly, back on the ship.

One of the big events of the Invergordon social season was the Inverness Gathering – Highland Games, balls and parties of all kinds. One of our senior mids was called MacGowan. He used to box professionally under a false name and was a colourful character. He was also laird of uncounted acres of Scottish moorland. He attended the Inverness Ball in full highland dress and so did Captain F. M. Austin, commanding HMS *Benbow*. They met in the bar and Captain Austin was most polite to the young laird, finally asking him to lunch the next day on board *Benbow* and failing to recognise one of his senior mids. I forget how it ended, but there was no lunch for MacGowan after he had been recognised on board the next day.

Rear Admiral John Casement, brother of the Irish spy executed in 1916, was one of the old school.[11] Nelson used to have his midshipmen to breakfast in the 'cuddy' so our admiral felt he should do the same. Eventually my turn came for this horrifying experience. I presented myself to the admiral and thereafter total silence ensued until he said, 'Don't let's stand about, let's have breakfast.' The five of us, admiral, flag captain, secretary, flag lieutenant and I, took our seats at a long table. The tablecloth was of purest linen, the napkins white and starched. Coffee was poured and I reached forward to pass the admiral the sugar. Unfortunately, the stiff white cuff of my best shirt caught the edge of my coffee cup and the contents spilled across the tablecloth. After a short silence the admiral called his chief steward and told him to clear the table. 'When you have re-laid the table we will start again.' Conversation was stilted for that long ten minutes but eventually the meal recommenced and my ordeal was over. 'Thank you, Sir, for a most enjoyable breakfast. It was kind of you to ask me.' It was not true, at least not the first part.

We continued our cruising until spring 1929 when we found ourselves in Gibraltar. The combined Mediterranean and Atlantic Fleets assembled there for manoeuvres at sea. It was during one of these that *Rodney* distinguished herself by firing a star-shell to port instead of starboard. Rather than illuminating the enemy ships beyond which the shells were set to explode, they silhouetted *Rodney* herself, to the amusement of both fleets.

Poor old *Rodney*, she was always in trouble. Unlike her sister ship, *Nelson*, *Rodney* was known as an unhappy and inefficient ship. During World War II she spent much time at Scapa Flow and many of her crew were desperate to get out of the Navy. This of course was impossible in wartime unless you were discharged with disgrace. That was the usual punishment for being caught in compromising circumstances with one of the sheep which abounded at Scapa. Some *Rodney* men took advantage of this quick road to civilian life and when *Rodney* went to sea she was greeted by every ship she passed with a loud 'Baa Baa-h-h'. One of the sailors charged with this particular offence endeavoured to excuse himself with the defence that he thought it was a Wren wearing a fur coat.

In Gibraltar we were involved in a tremendous sporting programme and took part in several parades ashore. We had landing parties of seamen from each ship who formed a battalion and were drilled on the racecourse by the fleet gunnery officer. It was at one of the march pasts that a certain lieutenant drew his sword only to have the blade break off at the hilt. Undeterred, he went through all the drill, waving the imaginary sword in a ceremonial salute, and was not bowled out by anyone.

Our section of five mids was transferred to HMS *Warspite*, flagship of Admiral Sir Frederick Field, in March 1929. *Warspite* was a much more modern ship than *Benbow* although she was old enough to have played a gallant part in the Battle of Jutland. There were several patches in the gunroom deckhead where shell holes had been repaired and we were proud to show these to our guests. There were also portholes so we at least had fresh air.

My greatest sporting triumph took place in the Combined Fleets Boxing Championships, in which I won the Officers' Lightweight. I have a cup to prove it too, though not a very big one. What happened was that the commander of *Warspite*, finding there were no officer entrants at this weight, had detailed me to enter and told me to find an opponent. I approached Midshipman Raikes, who was the right weight, and asked him if he would volunteer. He was most unwilling as he said he had never boxed. I finally persuaded him that all we had to do was to shuffle about the ring for three 1½-minute rounds to please the commander and uphold the honour of the flagship. I promised I wouldn't hurt him. My experience of boxing was fairly small but I had the advantage of having rather longer arms than average for my height. The coalsheds were packed for the occasion, the front rows gleaming with gold lace and boiled shirts and at the back serried ranks of sailors. My opponent did not have a very effective guard and temptation overcame me. I landed a beautiful uppercut to his chin. He dropped to the floor as if poleaxed and was counted out. The referee announced Midshipman Wingfield as the winner to loud applause. What a moment! Raikes was rather cross with me when he came to, but I apologised profusely and explained that it was a complete accident.

Another sporting success was in the Combined Fleets Regatta at Pollensa Bay, Majorca. In the officers' race, which was rowed in six-oared gigs, I was selected as bow for *Warspite*. This was an unusual position for me as the boat narrowed at the bow and I had difficulty with my arms. However, we trained hard and duly won by a canvas. A Tote was operated on one of the ships and there was a lot of money on each race. I had a day's pay (five shillings) on our crew and was delighted to collect a pound or two.

All through my mid's time I was very hard up. Most of my messmates had allowances from their parents, but I had to subsist on bare Navy pay of £91 a year. This went quite a long way in the 1920s. Cigarettes on board were 1s. 6d. for fifty and spirits were 1½d. a tot. Beer was the most expensive drink. I did not really suffer much privation and I certainly enjoyed my three years of gunroom life.

Commander Walter Fallowfield, second-in-command of *Warspite*, was an awe-inspiring figure. Scarlet-faced and portly, he ruled with a fairly heavy hand. He seldom went ashore and his wife did not accompany him to Malta. He said it wasn't worthwhile as he had to be on board at all times unless there was a ship's football match to watch ashore. He liked to give dinner parties in his cabin on the half-deck, which was where I slung my hammock. To entertain his lady guests after dinner, he would often order me to turn out of my hammock and then show the ladies how I got in again. I never thought this as funny as they did.

Once when we were cruising along the French Riviera it was decided to entertain the locals to a dance. This was a great feature of naval life at the time and a battleship quarterdeck made a fine ballroom. We were encouraged to dance at Dartmouth – with each other, of course, which would raise some eyebrows nowadays. Commander Fallowfield addressed us beforehand as follows:

'We are holding this dance to promote good relations with the local residents and to bring credit on the Royal Navy. It is important that *all* the guests should enjoy themselves. The duty of the midshipmen is to dance with the plain girls, the fat ones, the spotty ones, in other words, the wallflowers. The dance is not intended to be fun for you but you *may* have your reward. Sometimes these girls will have rich parents who will be delighted to see their ugly duckling enjoying herself. Perhaps Daddy will ask you to his house.'

The amazing thing was that this was exactly what happened to me. Daddy asked me to come riding with his daughter the next day. A car would pick me up at the landing at 10 a.m. I told him I would have to ask the commander for leave. This he was delighted to grant. 'Didn't I tell you it would happen?' he said triumphantly.

Life went on very happily for us in *Warspite*. We cruised the whole Mediterranean, calling at interesting places like Cannes, Monte Carlo, Athens, Venice, Algiers and Alexandria. The last was particularly enjoyable. We were taken by one of the local cotton magnates on a picnic to Aboukir Bay. He provided Arab ponies for us all and two charming daughters raced with us over the sand dunes. The history of the place, plenty of champagne, pretty girls and superb horses made it a notable day.

4

HAPPY DAYS IN THE GUNROOM (1929–31)

Early in 1930 HMS *Warspite* left Malta to join the Home Fleet (the new name of the Atlantic Fleet).[12] I took a photograph of Malta receding in the distance from the quarterdeck and captioned it in my album 'The best view of Malta'. I don't know why we mids disliked the island so much. Perhaps it was because we had spent so much time in dockyard hands repairing our turbines which had been damaged when we hit an uncharted rock in the Aegean. The blades were tipped and the rotors had to be removed for repairs. This was a big job, particularly as it had to be done by our own engine room department owing to an economy drive in progress at the Admiralty. Our section of mids became so fed up with sweltering in the dockyard that we wrote a formal letter to the captain asking if we could be appointed to the China Fleet. This was not well received. 'Young gentlemen must be content to serve wherever Their Lordships require them,' we were told.

On the way home we called for a week at Madeira which to my mind is a delightful place. We anchored in the bay so there was a lot of

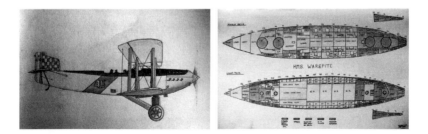

Illustrations from Wingfield's midshipman's journal

boat work in quite a noticeable swell. Several times the ship's boats had to be hoisted and we came off in the early dawn in a native boat. The gangways being also hoisted, we had to embark via the Jacob's ladder on the lower boom. I remember thinking it was rather incongruous doing this in a white tie and tails.

At Reid's Hotel one evening I got into conversation with a charming girl who introduced me to her parents, Sir Robert and Lady Bird of Bird's Custard fame. Pamela was an only child, it appeared, so she was something of a catch. I was longing to take her out to dinner but, alas, I only had a shilling or two in my pocket. The good Lady Bird must have guessed this as she discreetly stuffed a £5 note into my hand under the tablecloth. Off we went to the Casino, where I quickly won £10 at roulette. We had a nice dinner and I came back about £8 to the good. Pamela was a good dancer and quite fun, but I think she felt she could do a bit better than a midshipman. However, a couple of years later she married one of the *Warspite*'s mids. He retired young and they went to live in a Scottish castle.[13]

COWES (AUGUST 1930)

On joining the Home Fleet at Portsmouth we learnt to our pleasure that we were to be guardship at Cowes Regatta. This turned out to be the greatest fun and partially overcame the dislike of sailing which was inculcated in me at Dartmouth. What follows is based on a piece I wrote some years later for the *Royal Naval Sailing Association Journal*:

> Cowes Roads made a handsome picture during the first week of August 1930. The sun shone and the breezes were light. The latter was important because the J-class yachts, who formed the big attraction, seldom left their moorings if the wind was over Force 4. There were about six of these beautiful, if somewhat unseaworthy, craft. I remember *Britannia*, *Westward*, *Lulworth*, *Cambria* and *White Heather* and possibly *Shamrock*. *Westward* was too big for the J-class but raced with them.
>
> I was a midshipman in HMS *Warspite* and very proud to be able to point to a patch in the deckhead where a shell had

come through at the Battle of Jutland. As a change from endless tramping the teak as Midshipman-of-the-Watch, I was delighted to be allotted to an immense picket-boat which was attached to the Royal Yacht to help out her collection of ancient steamboats. (There is a splendid picture of one of these boats in an 1895 painting of Royal Yacht Squadron members which hangs in the drawing room at the Castle, Cowes.) One of our duties was to fetch the London evening papers from Southampton every afternoon.

This magnificent boat of mine was 56 feet long, single screw, coal fired and did 14 knots. Each morning we filled up with coal, carrying bags of the stuff down the port gangway. Then we scrubbed the gangway. I rather liked coal, having spent the previous year in HMS *Benbow* where we coaled ship every six weeks.

My boat had been brought out of reserve for Cowes Week and from the brass funnel, the carved teakwork and the quantity of brightwork it was easy to guess her origin. In fact the dockyard assured me she had been Lord Charles Beresford's barge when he was Commander-in-Chief Mediterranean before World War I.

She had, however, a most vicious kick when you went astern which was due to the large diameter of her screw. This caused difficulty when going alongside port gangways. One had to come in at a broad angle and go hard over at the last moment to swing the stern in before going astern. It was also necessary to use a fair amount of speed as she did not steer at all when going slow.

One day I was attempting to get alongside the *Victoria and Albert*'s port after gangway in a sluicing tide and not having much success. The officer of the watch, resplendent in frock coat and sword, started shouting advice to me from the top of the gangway. Vainly I struggled to make the brute go sideways. Then a regal figure wearing a toque and carrying a parasol who had been watching the proceedings turned to the officer of the watch and said, 'I think you had better leave him alone. He's probably doing his best.' Thank you Ma'am.

I remember the night of the Ball on board *Warspite*. All of us wore mess dress and very smart we looked in our round jackets and white waistcoats. If we were running a boat we wore dirks as well. I had to return several barge loads of champagne-happy guests to their yachts in the black dark without wrecking their flimsy gangways. Sir Philip Hunloke, the King's sailing master, stood beside me at the wheel and helped me identify the yachts.[14] He was worried that I might hit *Britannia*.

As well as *Warspite*, there were several smaller ships including a sloop whose job was to follow *Britannia* in case the King fell overboard. As none of the J-class had engines the sloop was often usefully employed towing them. There were warships from many nations including an antique looking vessel from the United States Navy with lattice masts which we rather disapproved of. Then of course there were the steam yachts, rather fewer and slightly smaller than in pre-war days (judging by the pictures), but a brave sight nevertheless.

We mids used to help crew the big yachts which always needed extra bodies to supplement their lavish complement of paid hands. I sailed in three of them including *Westward*. This great schooner was presided over by a terrifying character called T B Davis who had come up to wealth through the hawespipe, as we used to say. Life on board was not much fun while racing. He was his own skipper and certainly a fine seaman but his continual haranguing of the crew detracted from one's pleasure. The paid hands, sixteen of them, also used to mutter abuse at us for getting in their way.

About this time an immaculately dressed yachtsman watching the racing from the platform said 'Steward, that's a fine-looking yacht leading. Who's she?' 'She's yours, Sir Thomas,' was the reply. It was also said that Lipton, who never sailed his *Shamrocks*, had them painted green so he could recognise them.

One day on *Westward* there was an elderly gentleman standing aft and watching the proceedings as we laboured to haul in the sheets with enormous tackles running along the deck. There were of course no winches in those days. Davis shouted at him, 'Come on Admiral, get on that bloody sheet. I didn't invite you on board for the pleasure of your company.' Lord Jellicoe, for it was he, obediently joined us on the tackle.

A feature of the Week was Lady Baring's ball at Northwood House, which I scraped into somehow or other. It was, as they say, a glittering event. I danced like mad and got well stuck into the Bollinger. I even proposed marriage or something of the sort to a charming lady, but she told me gently that she thought she could do rather better than a Midshipman RN. She did too.

The sinking of the 12-metre *Lucilla* by *Lulworth* was an event which I watched from close range. I was in *Westward* and close ahead was *Lulworth* with *Britannia* in the lead. The wind was Force 5 on the quarter and we were thundering along westwards towards Cowes. With the number of sails we had up we were not exactly manoeuvrable; nearly out of control would have been a better description.

Out of the Medina River appeared the 12-metre, sailed by her paid hands only. (The owner and guests would be joining by launch at the 10-minute gun.) For some reason she took no avoiding action and was cut clean in half by *Lulworth*. *Lucilla* sank instantly, two of her crew being killed by the impact. The wreck is said to lie on the bottom just off the Squadron to this day.

Davis watched the collision with interest, remarking, 'There are plenty of boats to pick up the survivors. Now's our chance to catch *Britannia*.' Somewhere off Egypt Point we passed *Lulworth* floundering about in an effort to get back to the scene. In due course we passed *Britannia* and saved our handicap.

How the blame was distributed I don't know. It may have been one of those cases where the racing rules conflict with the Rule of the Road. There was of course a famous case of this at the start of the race off Dunoon about the turn of the century, when two enormous yachts collided. That case went to the House of Lords and cost the insurers a packet since all the lady guests claimed for masses of jewellery. I heard an eyewitness account of this incident from an aged yachtsman in 1955.

The big yachts had only a few more years of racing. A few of them are still afloat or used as houseboats. In the late 1930s I remember half a dozen of them laid up off Campers, while the mudflats off Blockhouse were littered with steam yachts whose day was done, but it was quite fun while it lasted. I don't personally feel many regrets. Sailing is a much healthier sport nowadays.

The RNSA cut out two pieces from my article. The first described a rather nasty accident which shook me at the time. Shoving off from Railway Jetty, Cowes, I rang down full speed and put the wheel over hard. The picket boat heeled violently and the coxswain overbalanced and fell overboard. The big propeller caught him and cut off his foot. I am afraid that was the end of his naval career. My first mention in the yachting press was unfortunate.

The other piece was about an important lady, Edwina Mountbatten. It was Regatta Sunday and the Bishop of Winchester was preaching to the royal family on the quarterdeck of HMY *Victoria and Albert*. Suddenly there was a roar of engines and from the Medina River appeared the fastest motorboat in the world, *Miss America*. Garfield Wood, the water speed record holder was giving Lady Edwina a taste of what we now call water-skiing, but was then known as aqua-planing.[15] Round the Royal Yacht they circled, Edwina calling shrill greetings to Uncle King and Auntie Queen. The Bishop's sermon went unheard as everybody peered at the slim and girlish figure in a two-piece bathing costume, cavorting gracefully behind the thundering engines of the world champion.

Lord Louis Mountbatten was a candidate for election to the Royal Yacht Squadron at the AGM the next day. He was not successful: one member said there were so many black balls he thought a rabbit must have got into the ballot box. Mountbatten did have another unsuccessful attempt at joining. He was proposed by King George V, who sent a note requesting that he be elected without further delay. The Squadron with one voice said they were not going to be pushed around by Buckingham Palace and blackballed him again. He never became a full member but he was an Honorary Member twice over, firstly as Chief of the Defence Staff and finally as Governor of the Isle of Wight.[16]

GREENWICH NAVAL COLLEGE

After my father's death in 1926 we had of course to leave Broome Rectory. My mother decided to build on a small building estate in Haslemere, Surrey. It was quite a nice house with four bedrooms and an attic, which was allocated to me. I think it cost about £3,000. My second elder sister was married at about this time to a missionary, but it did not turn out well. There was much religious activity and I was constantly pestered to take part in the Officers' Christian Union. I found its representatives, who were often in the house, most unattractive, but fortunately I was not often there.

In March 1931 we came to the end of our midshipmen's time and took the seamanship exam. This ranked high in importance. It was viva voce and the candidates were awarded a First, Second, Third or Pass Certificate. To my surprise and delight I was awarded a First. Later came a course at Greenwich Naval College, which was destined to give us a little taste of higher education. The old palace, and later hospital, was an architectural delight. We dined in the Painted Hall, which must be the grandest dining room in the world. The allegorical paintings on the ceiling made it hard to concentrate on the food. I was told that the artist, Thornhill, had difficulty collecting his fee from Charles II so he painted himself in the corner, holding out his hand. The silver and gold plate was fabulous and included a set of eight large silver salt cellars with the simple letters 'AR' on them. At least, there used to be eight but one night we gave a dinner to the officers of a visiting American ship, USS *Raleigh*. Afterwards there were seven and in some homestead in Texas a family may be wondering what 'AR' stands for.

Greenwich is pleasantly handy for the West End and we all took a more or less active part in the London Season. I had a car now, an open Triumph Seven, bright red, which was a thrill. After the Greenwich Ball, an important event of the Season, I and my friend Teddy Woodward took two girls and a few bottles of champagne all the way to the Ace of Spades on the Kingston Bypass, which we reached about dawn.[17] They kept open all night and were happy to let us drink our Bollinger NV out of coffee cups. One of the girls was a Miss Gradige, whose father made cricket bats and tennis rackets. She was getting on a bit, about twenty-seven I would say, but very pretty. She gave me a little encouragement but I had no wish to get married at twenty, and it was marriage or nothing with her, and with most of the other girls I met about this time. I take with a pinch of salt the tales of amorous successes related by my contemporaries. We were on the whole a virtuous lot, at least with women of our own class. Round the Portsmouth pubs it was a slightly different story.

I was not deeply involved in the London social whirl – I didn't have a penny more than my naval pay of about 14 shillings (70p) a day, so I couldn't afford to go to theatres or nightclubs much. However, I remember a few evenings at the Coconut Grove and the Kit-Cat and I suppose I was on nodding terms with Ambrose and his orchestra, Douglas Byng and Hutch. I was even in the company of the Prince of Wales once or twice. However, Peter Gregory, one of our term, was quite a Deb's Delight. He had several large cars, all bought for £5 or £10. Among them were a Delage, a Packard and a splendid old Bentley with straps round the bonnet and enormous copper pipes sprouting out of the side. He had a useful technique for getting in and out of college after the gates were closed at 11 p.m. In his car he carried running clothes and when he changed out of his white tie and tails (normal evening dress for the West End), he would present himself at the gate and explain that he had been out for an early morning training run in Greenwich Park. Not surprisingly he failed to get even a Third Class Certificate and was put back for another term. He explained to his parents that he had done so well that they had kept him on to help with the new intake of young officers. Later he joined the Fleet Air Arm, where he attracted some attention by having his cabin in the aircraft carrier *Furious* panelled in walnut by the shipwrights. Sadly, he was killed when the *Illustrious* was bombed by the Luftwaffe in January 1941. A charming and gallant officer.

I found the scholastic side somewhat beyond me, as usual, and only scraped through with a Third. The bright boys used to do the *Morning Post* crossword puzzle ostentatiously during lectures, but I know at least one who had to swot hard in the evenings in order to get the First which he duly received. It was considered rather bad form to show keenness on one's profession. A nonchalant, rather languid attitude to work was de rigueur and it was fashionable to despise anyone who showed a liking for mechanical or technical details. Although attributed to the Grenadier Guards, the axiom 'It is better to incur a mild rebuke than to perform an unpleasant duty', would have found much acceptance among our lot.

The Invergordon Mutiny occurred while we were at Greenwich. Amid much excitement the sub-lieutenants were organised into companies and armed with pick handles ready to combat any civil unrest. Greenwich was a hot Communist area and our commanding officer, Admiral Agar VC, was itching for what we would now call a confrontation – in plain words, a fight. Gregory and I went off one night in his vast Delage to listen to the speakers at a rabble-rousing meeting.[18] We seemed to attract some unfavourable attention from the throng and I was getting a little apprehensive when a policeman came up and said, 'I don't think they like people like you. Why don't you get away while the going is good?' We drove off while a few militants hammered on the bonnet.

About this time I joined the British Union of Fascists, led by Sir Oswald Mosley and supported by several Tory MPs. The only active part I took was as a steward or chucker-out at a mass rally in the Albert Hall. Everybody was most enthusiastic and the whole thing was great fun, although the expected Communists failed to appear, so we were not able to indulge in the strong-arm tactics for which we were prepared. Possibly these events formed a short paragraph in my dossier at MI5.

Other courses followed. I got a Second in navigation, a Third in torpedo and to my surprise a Second in gunnery. HMS *Excellent*, the gunnery school, had a fearsome reputation which was fully justified. At that time I was spending quite a few nights in London and driving back in the small hours ready to parade at 8 a.m. I suppose I was a bit sleepy on important occasions like Battalion Drill on Fridays, because I was warned that if I did not do better I might be failed. They seemed a humourless lot, our instructors. One day I arranged that when our platoon numbered we would call out 'One, two, three, etc., ten, Jack, Queen, King, Ace'. As a result we all had to double round the island, the standard punishment for misdemeanours. On another occasion we were being introduced to a new range-finder called the UB4. 'Ah,' I said, 'I've seen you before.' Loud laughter from the class, but an unfavourable reaction from the instructor. Gunnery in those days was the most important thing in the RN and was taken very seriously. Most of our senior officers were Whale Island graduates. I once commented on this disproportion among admirals and was told that the Gunnery branch only accepted the brightest officers and so it was natural that in the course of time they would have the most admirals.

Field guns competition, Wingfield is running by the right wheel, Whale Island, 1931

The Gunnery admirals were responsible for keeping battleships in the Fleet long after they had become useless liabilities. The invention of the torpedo, which enabled a destroyer and later a submarine or an aircraft to sink the strongest battleship, was the death knell. Previously only a battleship could fight a battleship. Not any more. Yet the Gunnery-dominated Admiralty kept on building more and more of them at vast cost. The last one, HMS *Vanguard*, went to sea after the end of World War II but only performed one useful function – acting as yacht for a royal tour of South Africa and Australia.

In submarines we had a poor opinion of surface ships' torpedo firing. At Jutland some hundred or more were fired, nearly all of which missed. In World War II the *Bismarck* was crippled by gunfire but our big ships were unable to sink her. Admiral Tovey ordered the *Dorsetshire* to sink her with torpedoes. Accordingly this fine cruiser steamed slowly past the largest warship in the world, which was stationary and burning, and fired her four portside torpedoes. All of them missed. She turned round and fired her starboard tubes and this time got a couple of hits. *Bismarck* then turned over and sank. Only a handful of survivors were picked up from this brave ship.

Somewhere in our family bloodstream must run a talent for passing exams. It certainly came out in the next generation as my two sons achieved some degree of scholarship. Anyway the result was that I achieved a Second in Gunnery right against the form book.

5

TRAINING FOR SUBMARINES (1931–33)

One could either specialise in one of the naval crafts like Gunnery, Torpedo, Navigation, Submarines, or the Fleet Air Arm, or be a non-specialist known as a 'salt-horse'. The latter would involve years of 'tramping the teak', i.e. watch-keeping in battleships or cruisers. Most of us had had our fill of this boring duty as midshipmen-of-the-watch. I opted for Submarines and have never regretted it. When I told my mother I had volunteered for this branch of the service she was not pleased. 'I hear they are a hard-drinking lot in submarines,' she said. I cannot think where she got this idea. I was reminded of her comment when I announced my determination to join the Navy: 'I am glad you are not going into the Army. It is an idle and dissolute life in peacetime. The Navy is more like a police force.' I suppose if you had spent some years in India before 1914, and then lost your eldest son in his first battle, you were likely to have an anti-army bias. I have always got on well with soldiers and have a feeling that I might have been quite happy with a military career if things had turned out differently. I think my mother carried it a bit far when she made a bonfire of all my father's military relics and souvenirs. There were bricks from old temples, banners, German cavalry lances and, saddest of all, my grandfather's shako (military cap) which he had worn in the Indian Mutiny. All destroyed. Only my father's medals survived.

BATTLESHIPS AGAIN

My application to join submarines, or rather take the submarine Training Class, was accepted but I had four months to fill in before

I joined the Submarine School. For this period I was appointed to HMS *Valiant*, one of the battleships which had played a leading part in the Mutiny of the previous year. There was a sort of punishment routine in force for the officers. Leave was very restricted and we were made to feel that the Mutiny was our fault. In fact, the cause of it was a flat reduction of 1 shilling (5p) a day in the pay of every officer and man. This was bearable for officers, but for the seamen, who were paid 4 shillings (20p) a day, it was the last straw. The whole board of the Admiralty should have resigned in protest at such a monstrously unfair economy measure, but they didn't and no one was sacked in Whitehall. Not so in the Home Fleet, where all the captains and their seconds-in-command had their careers blighted.

Admiral Joe Kelly was the new commander-in-chief and he brought with him a reputation for being a 'Jolly Jack', which was the term we used for one who sought to ingratiate himself with the lower deck by informality and over-familiarity with ratings. He ordered extra leave for all crews over Christmas 1932 and in *Valiant* we had only 80 men out of 700 on board. Even the cells were occupied by the wives of the small duty watch. There was no leave for the wardroom, gunroom or warrant officers and each mess was full for Christmas dinner.

The senior sub-lieutenant of the gunroom was the aforementioned Oliver Brocklebank, so with nothing to do, it is not surprising that we led a pretty riotous life. We were supposed to have our wine bills limited to £2 a month, but Brocklebank had found some way round the regulations, probably by inventing a few additional officers who, while non-existent, nevertheless consumed their full ration.

There was one amusing character in the wardroom, a lieutenant called Tommy Woodrooffe. Years later it was he who achieved world-wide fame by his broadcast account of Coronation Review at Spithead in 1937. There have been many replays of his description of the fire-work display, 'The Fleet's lit up', delivered in extremely slurred tones. I was on board my submarine at Spithead on this occasion and found it hilarious.

Woodrooffe was a practical joker and constantly in trouble. One evening at dinner in the wardroom a signalman came up to the commander and showed him a signal pad on which was written some quite appalling message. The commander's astonishment turned to rage when he recognised the signalman as Woodrooffe in disguise. 'Woodrooffe,' he roared, 'I am putting you under arrest.' 'But you can't do that, Sir.' 'Why can I not put you under arrest, may I ask?' 'Because I'm under arrest already, Sir!' It was some weeks before dear old Tommy Woodrooffe got ashore.

After a few more dreary months in the *Valiant* I was appointed to HMS *Dolphin*, Fort Blockhouse, Gosport, for training in submarines. I joined the Officers' Training Class in the summer of 1933.

SUBMARINES AT LAST (1933)

Blockhouse, as the submarine base is known, is not the grandest of the many naval establishments around Portsmouth, but it must be the oldest. It is said that a marauding fleet under the command of the Bishop of Caen was once forced to shelter from a gale in the snug harbour on the west side of the harbour entrance. 'God's Port' the Bishop christened it and Gosport it is to this day.

Sometime in the Middle Ages the piratical raids of the French corsairs made it necessary to fortify the entrance to Portsmouth harbour. Southsea Castle was built on one side and Fort Blockhouse on the other side at Gosport. In the early 1900s the first British submarines, the Holland class, were based at Blockhouse. The old Fort was continuously adapted to its new role and building never ceased. Nowadays submarines are a big growth business and new offices, workshops and accommodation blocks go up every year. There is an excellent museum where, in addition to a few souvenirs donated by the author, the visitor can see HM Submarine *Holland I*, rescued from the seabed after seventy years.

It was to this historic spot that I and seven other sub-lieutenants came to be taught the art and technique of submarining. First we had to meet the Rear Admiral Submarines who was none other than Martin Dunbar-Nasmith VC. He went down the line asking each of us why we wanted to join submarines. We knew what was expected of us and each replied that we wished to have responsibility when young, hoped for command early, and had a liking for things mechanical and electrical. (If we had been truthful we would have said that anything was better than the prospect of years of tramping the quarterdecks of battleships and cruisers.) Last in our line was Sub-Lieutenant Teddy Woodward. At least he was honest when he replied to the admiral's question: 'Because I want to get married and I need the extra money.' Dunbar-Nasmith was visibly displeased by such frivolity and Teddy took a long time to redeem his reputation. Ten years later, as captain of HMS *Unbeaten* based on Malta, Teddy notched up an impressive score of enemy sinkings and was awarded the DSO three times. His targets were mostly ships supplying fuel and ammunition to the Afrika Korps. The efforts of the Malta-based squadron contributed much more than has been generally recognised to the defeat of Rommel.

I was very happy at Blockhouse. Plenty of cheerful young officers – submarine enthusiasts to a man, a comfortable, indeed luxurious, mess, lots of seagoing and lots of shore-going. One of the local young ladies even inveigled me into taking a small part in amateur theatricals at the Gosport Theatre. I was, and am, quite hopeless as an actor and I found it quite impossible to embrace the leading lady with sufficient fervour. The *Portsmouth Evening News* put it well: 'Sub-Lieutenant Wingfield gave a restrained performance.'

It was not, however, my first experience of the stage. As a midshipman in Malta I had appeared at the Opera House, Valletta, in Gilbert and Sullivan's classic HMS *Pinafore*. I was one of the guard of marines who welcomed the First Lord. It was not a speaking part but we certainly sang the choruses. Another of the guard was a subaltern of the Highland Light Infantry called David Niven, who became a good friend. He took life light-heartedly and was often in trouble, but his charm, or charisma as we would now say, usually got him out of it. A night on the tiles with David was a memorable experience.

The commander-in-chief, Admiral Sir Frederick Field, decided to give a big formal dance at Admiralty House on a certain night. David Niven and another HLI subaltern called Trubshawe decided to give a dance on the same night at a casino on the seafront at Sliema. Invitations were sent out, caterers engaged and the famous dance band of the Rifle Brigade hired for the evening. To the surprise of the commander-in-chief, his guests started making their excuses and saying their goodbyes from ten o'clock onwards. By midnight there was only the flag lieutenant left, dancing with Miss Field. Everyone had gone on to David's party, which was an enormous success. Lady Field was said to be rather cross with David Niven.

I got on reasonably well in the Training Class but submarine electrics proved nearly incomprehensible to me. I could operate the main motors and charge the batteries quite efficiently but the theory behind it all was highly complicated and I now think irrelevant. I was certainly relieved, when I got command some years later, not to have to pretend any more that I knew *why* it all worked.

The teaching of navigation in my day was 80 per cent theory and 20 per cent practical. I firmly believe that it is a waste of time to spend hundreds of hours studying spherical trigonometry when all a navigator needs to know is how to take sextant altitudes of the sun and the stars and how to work out a position from these observations. Yet as midshipmen we were subjected to classes in navigation several times a week, taken by an instructor lieutenant who was good at maths but had never navigated a ship in his life. We had to produce a book containing only six examples of worked-out sights per year. No wonder the average naval officer is so markedly inferior to his opposite number in the Merchant Navy in astro-navigation.

Much the same might be said about the complicated business of adjusting a magnetic compass for deviation. There is no likelihood that anybody but a specialist would ever be required to do this, yet we spent scores of hours being taught the methods of removing the different errors. While we spent much time learning how to operate squadrons of battleships (someone described these manoeuvres as lumbering giants dancing quadrilles on the surface of the Mediterranean), we did not acquire a thorough knowledge of the Rules of the Road, or, more precisely, the Regulations for the Prevention of Collisions at Sea! In fact the pass mark in this subject was only 50 per cent. Merchant Navy officers learn the Rules by heart and can recite them with total accuracy. I believe they are required to get 100 per cent in this subject to receive a Mate's Ticket. This prompts the anti-naval jibe that if you meet a Royal Navy ship at sea it's best to watch out as there is a 50 per cent chance of the naval officer of the watch doing the wrong thing.

It is my view that by cutting out a large amount of theoretical study from the training of young officers, their practical efficiency could be greatly improved and much time saved. Let the specialists in Gunnery, Torpedo, Navigation, Electronics and Engineers be taught from first principles, but teach only what is necessary to the operators. In World War II the United States had to produce hundreds of ships' officers to man the Liberty Ships which were pouring out of the shipyards. By concentrating on *how* rather than *why*, they could turn a college boy into an adequate navigating officer in weeks rather than years. I am distressed to hear that recently the authorities have introduced engineering as a subject in the examination of masters and mates. In my view, engineering is best left to engineers, and the interference of the master, with the little knowledge that is so dangerous, in matters which are the sole concern of the chief engineer, is a recipe for trouble.

There was no vacancy for me in the frontline submarines when I finished Training Class, so I was appointed to the Reserve Submarine Squadron. These were worn-out relics of the Great War (as indeed were their commanding officers) and included some of the E-class and early L-class. There was also one of the experimental R-class with very high underwater speed but it was not a success in the anti-submarine role. Nobody pretended to do much work and the heaviest job that fell to me was wardroom wine caterer. The account books were chaotic and the stock contained such bizarre items as six dozen bottles of Angostura Bitters – enough for about 150 years. However, there were some nice pubs in the district including 365 Brickwoods houses in Portsmouth alone, many of which we investigated. One of the best was the Inn-by-the-Sea at Lee-on-Solent. This had a great reputation for the beauty of its barmaids and was a popular resort for submariners and pilots from the neighbouring Naval Air Station. Quite a few actually married the girls there and I am sure were happy ever after. There was a certain paymaster lieutenant who rejoiced in the unattractive name of Smellie.

He was lucky to find anyone to marry him and we all sympathised with the bride on having to become Mrs Smellie. But she had the last laugh: the young man rose to the top, got his 'K' and she became Lady Smellie.

Early in 1934 I embarked in the Blue Funnel liner *Patroclus* and twenty-eight days later, in Hong Kong, I joined HM Submarine *Odin* as 4th Officer.

6

ODIN AND THE CHINA FLEET (1933-35)

Our voyage out had been fun. It is sad that the slow boat to China, or anywhere else for that matter, scarcely exists any more. Long lazy days, no work to do, swimming and sunbathing, five-star menus in the dining room and cheap drinks in the bar, make for an idyllic four weeks. I suppose we got a bit bored towards the end because I remember one night when four of us sub-lieutenants decided to have dinner backwards. We started in the smoking room with brandy and coffee, then down to the saloon where we worked up the menu from ice cream to soup via roast lamb and fish, finishing up in the bar with a couple of pink gins.

HMS *Odin*, in which I was to serve for six years with a year's break in the middle, was one of a class of ocean-going submarines built

Submarine flotilla with depot ship HMS Medway

during the late 1920s. Although she had no air conditioning (it had not been invented), she was roomy and comfortable. The officers even had a miniature bath in which we usually kept blocks of ice and soft drinks.

For the next two years we cruised all over the Far East. Usually we were in company with our depot ship HMS *Medway*, a luxurious hotel for the submarine crews as well as a small floating dockyard. The junior officers learnt to handle their submarines from the start since the duty officer, who might be the sub-lieutenant, had to berth and re-berth the ship without any assistance from his seniors, if there was what was called a 'trot movement', that is, the inside submarine going to sea. If a gale blew up in the night and caused the submarines alongside *Medway* to bump, he had to cast off and anchor clear of the depot ship. I thoroughly enjoyed these occasions and developed what, with all modesty, I can describe as a fair ability to handle ships. Of course, submarines are the easiest of ships to manoeuvre, since they have very little windage and excellent brakes, that is, astern power.

The competition between the submarines was intense both in sport and in torpedo and gunnery exercises. All the commanding officers were in the zone for promotion to commander and only one in three in the whole Royal Navy made the step. I think it was unfair that the commanding officers of submarines, which were major war vessels, with several years' experience of command, had only the same chance of promotion as a lieutenant commander in a battleship whose finest hour was when he was allowed to operate the main derrick in the commander's absence. Some of the wives tried to help their husbands' chances by excessive social activity, but I don't think it did any good. I would go so far as to say that while a wife cannot help her husband's career very much, she can certainly damage it! One or two of them who found the gin bottle on the sideboard rather too handy were cases in point.

It would be tedious to relate our ports of call and describe our cruises in detail. There was not a major port in the Far East that we did not visit, plus a great many smaller ones. Weihaiwei was our summer base where we did some intensive exercising at sea and much strenuous exercise ashore. It was a delightful holiday resort with a perfect climate, where we played every game except rugby. The golf course with sand

The fleet at Weihaiwei

greens was something we had to thank our predecessors for. A little row of shops included Sin Jelly Belly, the tailor, some of whose clothes I wear to this day. His label inside my camel hair coat (coat £3 10s.) evokes happy memories. More sinister, although we didn't realise it, was Kodaka's camera shop. It turned out later that this smiling Japanese who developed our films was a naval officer whose duty was to keep an eye on the British China Fleet.

Just along the coast at Chefoo was a small United States Navy Base. A flotilla of very ancient submarines and a division of World War I destroyers were a laughing stock to us with our modern fleet, but we were on friendly terms with their officers. They were somewhat embarrassed socially by the fact that their ships were dry. This was nothing to do with Prohibition but dated from 1910 when Secretary of the Navy Daniels had closed the bars in all US ships. In imitation of our rum tubs with 'God Save the King' in brass letters, one American captain had his chippies make a similar one labelled 'God damn Josephus Daniels'.

A bit further north was Chinwangtao, which we visited once for ten days (a good feature of pre-war naval cruises was that visits lasted a week or ten days, allowing one to get to know the local British colony better – nowadays it is two days, at the most three). There was a train to Peking and I am privileged to have stayed a few days in that glorious city, not yet under Communist rule. I clicked my camera at the Forbidden City, the Great Wall and the Summer Palace. The air was so clear and the sun so bright that all the pictures came out well. I remember my father had told me that Great-uncle Alfred had been among those who sacked the Summer Palace after the Boxer Rising and got away with one of the Empress Dowager's bedroom slippers encrusted in pearls. 'If you are looting,' said my father, 'only go for small things. Anything big like pictures or tapestry is a waste of time as you will never get them home. Jewels are best.' He would obviously have approved of the green eye of the little yellow god.

We had a polo match at Chinwangtao between *Odin* and our 'chummy-ship' *Otus*, which had some unusual features. Chinese ponies were plentiful; there were always a few at the foot of the gangway, and we used them instead of rickshaws, so we had no trouble mounting our teams of eleven-a-side. Using hockey sticks and a football we had a hilarious game. The ponies thoroughly disapproved, many of the sailors being carried far from the scene of the struggle and deposited in paddy fields.

Japan was a popular port of call with us. I only went to Kobe, but we saw quite a bit of this fascinating country. It is hard to believe that in the mid-1930s golf was little known in Japan. There were a few courses, mostly supported by the European community, but there was no sign of the golfing explosion which has since taken place. I played at Hirona, a beautiful and almost deserted course where the turf was said to have been imported from California; also at the Kobe Club where I had the bad luck to hit a Japanese with a golf ball at a blind hole. There was an appalling row, the secretary was called and I had to apologise over and over again. It was the same club where I saw a Japanese shank his drive so badly that it hit his caddy and knocked him out. Quite unmoved, he called to the caddy master for another caddy. 'This one is not good,' he said, or words to that effect.

I had a favourite caddy at Weihaiwei called Ah Chee. I thought he would be a help on board so I 'bought' him from the caddy master for ten dollars, about £1. He was known as 'makee-learn' and worked in the wardroom galley. Gradually he became more and more my personal 'boy' and eventually became an official locally enlisted Officer's Steward. He was devoted to me and when, several years later, I finally left *Odin* in Malta he asked to go home. 'You go England. I go China-side.' Alas, this could not be arranged but I promised him that after just one patrol he would be sent back to North China. Sadly he was lost with the rest of the crew on their first Mediterranean patrol. I still think of him with affection.

Java was another popular cruising area. The Dutch were good colonists and had no colour bars. Unlike the British in India they tended to make their permanent homes in the Netherlands East Indies. The islands

Ah Chee on HMS Odin

were incredibly rich in natural resources and produced almost everything. At one golf club I remarked on a small oil-derrick beside the 9th green. 'Very useful,' said my Dutch friend, 'Every golf club should have one.' Now as I sit at my desk I can see on the mantelpiece two superbly carved Balinese heads which I bought for a few dollars. One day we were taken on a trip to the more or less extinct volcano called Mount Bromo.[19] After a couple of hours' drive we left the car and proceeded across the Sandzee, which was the inside of the old crater, on horseback. At the centre was a fifty-foot hole where a lot of hot lava could be seen, rumbling gently with occasional puffs of sulphur.

As submariners we were rather envious of the Dutch submarines, which were fitted with schnorkels.[20] These were long tubes which could extend just above the submarine so that the submarine was virtually invisible but could still draw in air for the diesel engines. The Germans copied this device and used it with great effect during World War II. It was not until very late in the war that our submarines were fitted with it.

As can be imagined, Singapore and Malaya were happy hunting grounds with many superb golf courses. In *Odin* we called at a place called Port Dickson where I witnessed the raising of a regiment. The government decided that it would be a good idea to have a Malay Regiment and accordingly sent a colonel, a major and a sergeant to Port Dickson, where they set up a table in the main street and invited the locals to enlist. The Malays, unlike the Chinese who outnumbered them in Malaya, are not very keen on hard work but love uniforms and parades. They filled the quota of 800 men quite easily and very smart they looked in their green and khaki dress. I believe they fought quite well in the war but were given a bad time by the Japanese after the fall of Singapore.

Another place we visited was Port Swettenham. Here we entertained the local chief of police on board at lunchtime. He was a portly man, and without air conditioning it can be imagined that the heat gave him a powerful thirst. At about 2.45 p.m. I gently suggested he might like to go home to his lunch. 'Oh no,' he said, looking at the depth gauge. 'It's only a quarter to one. I'd love another gin.' I turned to Ah Chee and said, 'OK, let's have something to eat.' 'Yes, master,' he replied. 'Which you want, lunch or tea?'

In spite of all our cruises we spent most of the winter months in South China, mostly at Hong Kong. One night at the Hong Kong Hotel, known for some reason as The Grips, an army friend who was dining with a few of us had the chit he signed for his dinner returned by the head waiter. Apparently he had run out of credit. He wanted to borrow from us but none of us were very keen until he offered the use of his pony every other Saturday for the season in return for the cost of his meal. I jumped at this and so got my first and only experience of hunting. Once a fortnight I dressed myself in breeches and bowler and went out by train to Fanling. (I should have mentioned earlier that while at Greenwich I had done an equitation course at the Military Academy, Woolwich, and so could ride reasonably well.) It was a drag hunt and for an hour or so we trotted and cantered over dried up paddy fields and jumped Chinese tombstones. David Gregory, brother of Peter, was well mounted and always up with the hounds. On my first day I innocently asked him if he had won. With withering scorn he informed me that it was a hunt not a race and there were no winners.

HMS Odin

Odin *wins gunnery competition, summer 1935 (10 hits in 65 seconds starting from periscope depth; first round in 21 seconds)*

Later he rose to vice admiral and on retirement became custodian of some ducal castle where I am sure he enjoyed himself.[21]

I won my very first golf prize about this time (1935). I was playing off 16 then (as indeed I am now, after thirty-five years on 12), and managed to collect the Tamar Tankard, which looks very handsome in my rather sparsely furnished trophy cabinet. Much more important was winning the gunnery competition or Captain Submarines' Firing Cup.

I had by this time taken over responsibility for gunnery in *Odin* and worked hard training the gun's crew. Briefly, the competition involved surfacing, firing ten rounds at a target and diving again. We won with a good score but nothing like as fast a time as we were to achieve in later years. However, the success did my self-esteem a power of good.

In 1935 we experienced a severe typhoon in Hong Kong. We had plenty of warning and had time to move from alongside *Medway* to buoys in the harbour where we dived and sat on the bottom in perfect safety. When it was over we surfaced and witnessed an extraordinary scene of destruction. Twenty-five ships of over 1,000 tons were stranded, one of them with its bows right across the waterfront. The losses among the junks ran into hundreds. The barograph trace showed the pressure dropping at a steep angle until it ran off the paper and rose equally sharply when the storm centre had passed. On shore one embarrassing consequence of the rapid alteration in atmospheric pressure was that the sanitary system started to work in reverse and the toilets became fountains, flooding many houses.

In early 1936, after an enjoyable P&O liner voyage, I returned to England. After six weeks' foreign service leave I was appointed first lieutenant of HM Submarine *H.50* commanded by Lieutenant J. D. Luce, later to be Admiral Sir David Luce, First Sea Lord of the Admiralty.

7

WAR ON THE HORIZON (1936-40)

On 25 July 1936 at Lynchmere Church near Haslemere, Surrey, I was married to Sheila Leschallas, daughter of Major John Leschallas of Lynchmere House. The wedding was a big affair and the description of the presents and list of guests covered three columns of the *Haslemere Herald*. I and my best man Anthony Collett wore naval full dress with cocked hats and swords, as did the half

Marriage to Sheila Leschallas, 25 July 1936

Wedding present from Major Leschallas, a Wolseley 10

dozen officers who came up from the submarine base at Portland to support me. As is the naval custom, the depot ship HMS *Alecto* hoisted a garland between the masts in celebration of the wedding. Later I was amused to see that I had been charged £1 10s. on my mess bill for the flowers. It is satisfactory to look around me now and see how many of the wedding presents are still in use, notably a trolley table which we must have used for supper nearly every day for forty-seven years.

Our honeymoon was short, as two days after the wedding my submarine had to sail to Chatham to take part in Navy Week. This was rather fun as it was a mock battle between Chinese pirates in a junk and the submarine, which surfaced and shelled it. We had a problem simulating the explosive charges, which could be electrically detonated, round the conning tower. The difficulty was keeping the charges dry when we dived. I am proud to say I found the solution in a local chemist's shop where I bought 200 rubber devices which were the perfect answer. 'Have a nice weekend,' said the chemist cheerily as he ushered me out.

In November the Home Fleet, assembled at Portland, was visited by King Edward VIII. No suspicion of future events marred the occasion. It would be difficult to imagine a more popular monarch. He was enthusiastically cheered by the Fleet and by the public ashore. I was presented to him at a reception on board the aircraft carrier HMS *Furious*, and we chatted for five minutes or so. He had charisma in a marked degree as well as youthful good looks. I particularly remember his light gold hair, slightly wavy, and his rather nasal accent which was well reproduced by Edward Fox in *Edward and Mrs Simpson*, Thames TV, 1978.

We were stunned by the Abdication on 6 December. If the King had decided to fight for his throne he would have had the whole Fleet behind him and a sizeable portion of the British people. I know I would have drawn my sword in his defence without hesitation. Wisely perhaps, he decided to depart quietly, thus avoiding a civil war.

An enjoyable feature of our training programme was a simulated war in the Sea of the Hebrides. All the Home Fleet submarines, including eight or nine H-class, were placed in patrol areas, through which targets of different sorts steamed by day. (Night operations were considered too dangerous.) We fired torpedoes with dummy warheads which clearly showed when they had hit the target. Looking back, I

Loading a torpedo

57

think these exercises were well conducted and good training for war. Unlike so many servicemen who complained that they were trained for the wrong war, I found that our training in peacetime worked well when put to the test.

In early 1937 I received an appointment to HMS *Odin* as first lieutenant. This was good news as I liked the ship and knew her well. After the usual happy four-week voyage, this time in the P&O ship *Rawalpindi*, I joined *Odin* at Hong Kong. Nothing had changed much and many of the crew were old friends from my previous appointment.

My wife Sheila soon joined me, having come out in another P&O ship. It is interesting to recall that in those days there were no marriage allowances and no free passages for wives to foreign stations. In fact my father-in-law paid the £50 P&O fare. We set up house in a flat near the naval hospital overlooking Wanchai, which was reached by a flight of about 100 steps. You could if you wished (I never did) have a chair for a few pence and be carried up the steps by two sweating coolies. Ah Chee joined us at the flat as *Odin* was in dock for a few weeks and we also had an amah and a cook-boy. I remember remarking to Sheila that I doubted if we would ever live so well again.

The exchange rate for the Hong Kong dollar was favourable so the cost of living was low. We went out a lot, often to the Hong Kong Hotel where the head waiter, a White Russian named Olevinski, was an old friend. The popular drink was a gimlet, consisting of gin, lime juice and ice, well shaken up and served in a flat champagne glass – delicious in the hot and humid climate of South China.

We had a friend at this time called Alistair Drummond, who was a chartered accountant and

Amah

doing very nicely in the frantic financial rat-race of the boom town of the Far East. He had a small yacht in which I had some pleasant sails. In Hong Kong even then there was much talk of the political risks but this did not deter the local developers. It was, and probably still is, one place where you can make a fortune in ten years.

We cruised all round South East Asia. At Saigon in Indo-China, then under French colonial rule, we enjoyed some good sightseeing. Sheila went with a friend to Angkor Wat, the recently discovered palace in the jungle which must be one of the wonders of the world.

Gunnery went well too. I took up training our gun's crew where I had left off a year before. We won the Captain Submarines' Firing Cup with a record score. The first round was fired 21 seconds after breaking surface. We scored hits on the target with all ten rounds and were dived again in 57 seconds after surfacing. I used this technique many times in the war years with great success. Sometimes we sank the ship before she had even manned her guns. It was good sport and good training.

Our happy life was interrupted in 1938 when the Munich crisis blew up. We hoisted the warheads out of the magazine and fitted them on the torpedoes. A few weeks later we put them back in the magazine and carried on cruising. But not for long. On 1 September 1939 Sheila and I were in the cinema in Singapore when a notice on the screen said, 'All naval personnel return to your ships forthwith.' Germany had invaded Poland.

I went back to the naval base to find the ship busy storing for war. 'Nice of you to turn up,' said the captain, 'we've been hard at it for six hours.' That night we sailed and steamed at full speed to Penang only a short way up the coast of Malaya. I was duty officer on 3 September and was the recipient of the laconic signal from the Admiralty, 'Total Germany', which being interpreted meant 'Commence hostilities against Germany'.

I looked around but there didn't seem to be much I could do. I felt there was a need to dramatise the occasion so I told the duty petty officer to pipe 'Clear Lower Deck'. The chief engine room artificer asked if he should stop charging the batteries, to which I agreed. The duty watch shuffled on deck and stood around disconsolately. Mounting the gun platform, I said, 'This is an important announcement. We have received instructions from the Admiralty to commence hostilities against Germany. That means that we are now At War.' There was no reaction from my small audience. For good measure I added, 'The King's Regulations and Admiralty Instructions applicable in time of War ... er ... now apply.' This was a bit of an anti-climax but I needn't have worried. The hangdog expressions of the crew never changed. 'All right, petty officer, fall out the men.' Much of the duty watch returned to their bunks to complete their siesta. 'Can I put the charge back on again now, Sir?' asked the chief engine room artificer.

All the other officers were ashore at the Penang Club. I sounded the siren six times, which brought them hurrying on board in a sampan. We had a few drinks in the wardroom and the other lieutenant said he would take the duty so I could go ashore. At the club I was buttonholed by an elderly member who said, 'I advise you to watch out. I was in this club in 1914 when a German raider attacked the port and sank everything in sight.' Nothing, however, disturbed our peace. After a couple of games of golf, and a farewell party at which the old planters at the club deplored the fact that they were too old to fight, we sailed on our first war patrol.

WAR BEGINS (1939–40)

A peaceful voyage across the Indian Ocean took us to Colombo, Ceylon, where we joined a small flotilla based on HMS *Lucia*. This relic of World War I had been captured from the Germans in 1916 and roughly converted to the role of Submarine Depot ship. She had a native crew, each department being of a separate race. Owing to their religious rules, this necessitated five or six separate galleys where the correct food could be prepared and served, uncontaminated by infidel hands. All these little galleys ran on culinary coal, or coke, which caused some trouble later in the war when *Lucia* arrived at the American naval base of Guam. As was customary, she had signalled her requirements on arrival – bread, meat, water, etc. and concluding with 10 tons coke. Soon after anchoring, a lighter came alongside with a mountain of cartons on deck. Each carton contained two dozen cans of Coca-Cola.

Lucia's ship's officers were typical of those found in depot ships of all kinds from Sierra Leone to Scapa Flow. Not being fighting ships or given to much seagoing, the officers tended to be elderly, retired and of bibulous inclination. Certainly when I entered *Lucia's* wardroom at 4.30 the day we arrived, I was a little surprised to be immediately offered champagne by a couple of dugout commanders who must have missed Nelson only by a dog-watch.

Coaling ship in Colombo was light work for the crew. Lighters moored alongside and an army of natives, many of them women, carried the coal in baskets on their heads, up narrow planks to the coaling ports where they tipped it into the bunkers. A quite surprising tonnage per hour was achieved despite the great heat. At noon they all settled down to curry, the aroma of which was quite delicious. I, of course, was able to instruct my shipmates on the finer points of coaling.

Sheila arrived some time before Christmas in a Japanese liner called *Argentina Maru*. We set up house in a private hotel near the race course.

Odin did two or three patrols from Colombo. They were in fact rather like peacetime cruises, although the German battleship *Graf Spee* was suspected of being around somewhere. So we kept a good lookout and darkened the ship at night. *Graf Spee* was in fact in the South Atlantic, as we were electrified to hear when the news of the Battle of the River Plate broke. It was nice to hear some good news, as the phoney war period was one of severe losses to our submarines.[22] One day in September we lost three and we even had one captured intact by the Germans.[23]

I took my dinner jacket and golf clubs on these patrols and used both frequently. We called at most of the islands, including Mauritius where they produced a very palatable light rum. The Seychelles were the high point, however. At that time they were undiscovered by the world and, being served only by a steamer once a month from Mombasa, they had few visitors. It was a real semi-tropical paradise complete with waving palms, white beaches and beautiful light brown native girls. I met the secretary of the local club, who described what a happy life he led on the £10 a month remittance which his parents sent him. Apparently he had been cashiered from the RAF for some unmentionable offence which caused his father to insist that he stayed out of England.

He asked me if I would like to make a bit of money and pointing to the primitive huts which lined the seafront said, 'You can have any of that land for £40 an acre. Some day it might be valuable.' I turned down his kind suggestion, as it seemed pointless to spend money on land in an island with no communications. Today the big jets bring in hundreds of sun-lovers from all over Europe and the seafront is lined with towering hotels.

One day some of the crew were fishing and were successful in catching six sharks on one hook. On hoisting up the shark and slitting open its belly, five young sharks jumped out and swam away with surprised expressions. We used to catch turtles sometimes and we did our best to eat turtle steak. It didn't even make very good soup. Sometimes there were forty or fifty eggs inside but fish-flavoured eggs were not for us. What these lumbering creatures did produce was turtleshell of great beauty. At lunch today we used a salad spoon and fork which I bought during *Odin*'s time at Mahé.

The Governor of the Seychelles was Sir Arthur Grimble who later wrote a bestseller called *A Pattern of Islands*. He had served many years in the South Pacific and West Indies and had a fund of stories which he told with great wit. His voice became familiar to radio audiences after his retirement, when he did an immensely popular travel series. Sir Arthur was very hospitable to *Odin*'s officers, but Government House was a disgrace to the British Empire. The paint was peeling, the verandas rotting and the bamboo furniture infested with nasty little bugs which bit our bare legs unmercifully. My armchair actually collapsed when I sat on it. I suppose we really had too many overseas possessions and had lost the will to maintain them properly.

One day at sea I received the news of my mother's death as a result of a fall at the house of her brother Crosbie Trench. She slipped on a rug on a polished floor and broke her hip. Nowadays the surgeons would have put this right in no time, but not in those days. She developed pneumonia and died in November 1939.

I never saw her will, but apparently she left all her nicest things to her daughters. The sons in South Africa and the Far East were unlucky and received few of the Wingfield relics. My share was a small quantity of Powerscourt silver, crested and coroneted, and the family dining table, a handsome piece of furniture which my mother had brought from her old family home in Kerry. Much to my regret I heard later that my sister had put it in the sale. Mother's house was nicely positioned in the Petworth Road, Haslemere. It was sold by auction for £3,500. I should have bought it but I was too far away.

In January 1940 we sailed for Malta and the real war began. The 10th Submarine Flotilla was based ashore at Lazaretto and conducted operations all over the Mediterranean against Italian shipping. The submarines were really too large and too easily detected in the calm and crystal-clear water, and there had been heavy losses.

My relief as first lieutenant joined at Malta and I left _Odin_ with sadness after six happy years in a fine ship.

Alas, _Odin_ did not return from her first Mediterranean patrol. It is believed that she was jumped by Italian destroyers while charging batteries on the surface at night. What may have happened is that the officer of the watch sighted something and called the captain to the bridge. Fresh from the bright lights of the wardroom he would have been night-blind and probably did not see until too late that most frightening of sights, the V-shaped bow-wave of an enemy destroyer coming straight at him. Lessons learnt the hard way in the North Sea had not been passed on to Malta. The officer of the watch must dive immediately without waiting for the captain's permission, and those due to go on the bridge should wear red-tinted goggles for at least fifteen minutes before going up. In addition, all lighting down below should be red as this does not cause night-blindness. None of this was practised in the Mediterranean in early 1940.[24]

HOME AGAIN (MAY 1940)

A short sea voyage from Malta to Marseilles in a P&O en route to

England was the start of a quite interesting journey. In peacetime it was common practice to go overland from Marseilles in order to gain a few extra days' leave, while the liner was lumbering through the Bay of Biscay. I didn't see why I should not adopt this custom, although the German armies were already advancing. It was comforting to know that the ports of the Maginot Line were impregnable. Indeed they were, but the Germans had unfairly outflanked them and gone through Belgium, where there were no defences.

Thus during our three-day train journey to Cherbourg we saw some strange sights. One unit of the French army we saw was marching steadfastly to the rear, without rifles and led by a fat major on a lady's bicycle. My travelling companions were the 1st Battalion of the Scots Guards. If you want a pleasant journey I can recommend them as cicerones. Three times a day there was a great stamping in the corridor and a couple of enormous guardsmen handed out the table d'hôte: onion soup, entrecôte de veau, wild strawberries, the lot. We established our rough whereabouts from the labels on the wine bottles which we bought at the stations. When they said Macon and then Sancerre and finally Muscadet we knew we were getting near the Channel.

At Cherbourg a sorry mess of defeated soldiers – Dutch, Belgians, even Norwegians I think – were all awaiting transport to England. No guns, no country, no hope.

Needless to say the Scots Guards had it all organised and in no time we were landing in Southampton with all our baggage. I remarked to the adjutant, a high-class soldier who masked his professionalism by a diffident manner, how the battalion managed to live so well under what were difficult circumstances. 'Mervyn, we have a saying in the Regiment – any bloody fool can be *un*comfortable!'

I had a curious experience during the Channel crossing. My cabin mate, an RNR lieutenant commander, told me in all seriousness that he could pinpoint the position of mines by extra-sensory perception. He had been in charge of the port of Calais and when the Germans dropped mines in the harbour he embarked in his motorboat complete with hazel rod and had no difficulty in locating and marking the mines, which could then be neutralised by divers. He showed me his chart with red crosses marking the positions. He then told me something which I repeat for what is it worth. He said that he found it was not necessary to go out in his boat – he could do it just as well over a large-scale chart in his office. Apparently he held some metal in his hand, concentrated his mind on mines and the hazel rod quivered over the exact spot on the chart.

This was a little hard to swallow but my friend was deadly serious. I suggested he might be able to detect U-boats in the North Sea, which would be really useful. He said he would be delighted to try. I heard the Admiralty gave him a trial and he confidently located several U-boats in Portland Harbour. As it was well known that there was a flotilla of our own submarines based at Portland, Their Lordships were not impressed.

I wrote an account of this man's claims for *The Naval Review* which attracted some interest.[25] I had a dozen letters from fervent believers in ESP asking for more details but there was little I could tell them.

8

EARLY WARTIME SUBMARINE
OPERATIONS (1940–41)

PERISCOPE COURSE AND *H.43*
(JUNE – NOVEMBER 1940)

My foreign service leave was spent at my wife's family home, Lynchmere House, near Haslemere. It was glorious weather but the news was alarming. The Dunkirk evacuation was just starting so, as I felt I could be useful, I telephoned Submarine Headquarters and asked if I could help out at Dover. 'On no account,' I was told. 'We are extremely short of Submarine COs and we cannot afford to waste any.' So I sat out Dunkirk in comfort, feeling rather a fraud. I now wish I had gone anyway. The staff at the ports were very hard-pressed and I am sure I would have been welcome.

I joined the Local Defence Volunteers, predecessors of the Home Guard, of which my father-in-law, Major Leschallas, was commander. He made a fine figure with his Boer War and Great War medals, scarlet complexion and white moustache. We received some boxes of rifles, which had to be degreased, and a few rounds of ammunition. When the church bells rang signalling that an invasion had taken place, I and my brother-in-law took up a defensive position in the churchyard and prepared to repel the German army. Fortunately it was a false alarm. Some of our own aircrew had baled out over Brighton and been mistaken for German paratroopers.

Invasion precautions were taken pretty seriously at that time. Most people expected Hitler to have a go at Britain and in some ways I think it was a pity he didn't. He could probably have put a few divisions ashore from barges but with the whole Home Fleet available, plus the RAF, I think he would have found resupply impossible. As Churchill said: 'London, if resolutely defended street by street, could swallow up an army.'[26]

My leave was short and I was soon off to Fort Blockhouse for the Commanding Officers' Qualifying Course, commonly called the periscope or 'perisher' course. We used the attack Teacher ashore to simulate the movements of an enemy which we observed through a periscope. The trick was to manoeuvre your submarine so that it was two or three hundred yards off the enemy's track and pointing in the right direction for firing the torpedoes.

Unlike all others, British torpedoes only ran straight. Our allies and enemies could angle their torpedoes so that after firing they turned to the desired course. This made the attack problem much easier, especially against a zigzagging target. It is strange how unsuccessful we have been in torpedo design. There have been plenty of bright ideas but all have failed in service. Thus when HMS *Conqueror* sank the Argentine cruiser *Belgrano* in 1982, she fired Mark VIII two-star torpedoes – the identical torpedo in use in *Odin* when I joined her in 1934.

For our sea training in real submarines against live targets we were based at Fowey. On the way there, we were changing trains at Reading when we saw on a newspaper placard 'FRANCE FALLS'. Our general reaction was one of relief. There was nobody now to let us down. To be on our own against the mighty Axis was an exhilarating thought.

Gradually we acquired the necessary skills for the exciting sport of submarine warfare. Our instructor or Teacher Captain was one Pat Steele, who was immensely experienced as a peacetime CO. He was on patrol in the North Sea in the early weeks of the war when he sighted a U-boat which he promptly torpedoed and sank. Unfortunately it was not a U-boat but a British submarine which had strayed out of its allotted area. Pat was judged blameless as it is virtually impossible to distinguish one type of submarine from another. All conning towers look much alike. The first lieutenant of the attacked British submarine was an old friend called Pat Coppinger, whom we much missed.[27]

When our shortened periscope course was completed, we were appointed to our first commands. Mine was to an ancient World War I vintage boat called *H.43*. She was really quite unfit for this war, but our losses had been heavy and Mr Churchill insisted that we patrolled the Heligoland Bight. I joined the flotilla at Harwich and was soon on my way to a patrol area off the Dutch coast. I was supposed to rendezvous with Dick Coltart on his way back from the area but he didn't turn up. He had in fact been sunk a few days earlier.[28] There was very little traffic through my area so one might say that the submarine policy was successful in stopping sea trade even if our toll of enemy shipping was small. I fired a couple of torpedoes at some barges with little hope of hitting. They were of such shallow draught that I expect the torpedoes ran underneath. I also stalked a U-boat for some time but as the light improved it turned into a short, stubby lighthouse on the shore. All quite exciting and good experience. We did not encounter any anti-submarine craft but judging by the distant bangs, some of our colleagues did. I was to be relieved on patrol by another old shipmate from China days. However, he also failed to arrive and I heard later that he had struck a mine.[29]

HARWICH, BLYTH AND SHEERNESS (NOVEMBER 1940 – APRIL 1941)

There was a rather subdued air about the submarine base at Harwich. Successes had been few and there were too many empty seats at the breakfast table. The shallow waters of the southern North Sea were really quite unsuitable for submarine operations, particularly when the submarines were out of date and the anti-submarine forces highly efficient. I did a couple more patrols quite uneventfully before we were ordered to go up the coast to Blyth where another small submarine base had been established. However, before leaving Harwich we had one incident which relieved the gloom.

One day a large black car with a uniformed chauffeur drew up outside the office of the captain. An elderly lady disembarked, followed by a gangling youth of about twenty. Demanding to see the captain, she announced that they were the Dowager Countess of Craven and the Earl of Craven. 'My son wishes to join the Navy and would like to serve in a submarine. I hope you can find a place for him in one of your boats,' she said.

The captain tried to explain that the boy would first have to join as a rating, then achieve promotion to sub lieutenant and then do a submarine training course, but the Countess was not impressed. 'Surely it makes a difference when he is an earl. Please do try and fit him in, Captain, he would so love to be a submariner.'

I remember little of Blyth except that some of the boats based there were French and owed their loyalty to de Gaulle. We envied them their wine tank. Only in a dire emergency was the order given 'Videz le vin rouge.'

Earlier in the year I had taken part in the transfer of the French fleet to British custody. At Portsmouth there was the battleship *Paris*, some destroyers and a few submarines.[30] I had no trouble with the one I took over but on the *Surcouf* there was a shoot-up in the wardroom. One of the French officers drew a pistol and shot dead the British commander and a lieutenant. He in turn was killed by our petty officer. The French crew then surrendered. Nearly all the French officers and men in Britain opted for a return to France rather than the alternative of joining de Gaulle and the Forces Françaises Libres. It must have been an agonising choice for disciplined men devoted to their country. I am glad that I never had to make such a decision.

I was pleased to leave Blyth. The little group of wives and children at the gate of the submarine base, waiting for news of an overdue submarine, became rather depressing. We called briefly at Dundee, where the submarine base was once again established in the marmalade factory which it had occupied during World War I. The submarines were mostly Dutch and our relations with this ally were always very warm. Their submarines were clean, efficient and very successful. So good was their command of the English language that they dispensed with liaison officers when working with our fleet. Not least in their favour was their rijsttafel, an immense Indonesian curry which they always had on Sundays. Not so much a meal as an afternoon's occupation, we used to say. (I first had rijsttafel at the Hotel des Indes in Batavia, Java. The side dishes were brought in by twenty-four waiters and consisted of every kind of spice to make you hot, and bananas and gula melaka [sago pudding] to cool you down. Punkahs overhead provided a welcome current of air).

We continued northwards, through the dreaded Pentland Firth, calm on this occasion, and on to the Clyde, which I was to come to know very well. The job of the flotilla here was to provide targets for the Anti-submarine School, a dreary but necessary task which we called clockwork mouse. One of the small ports we used was Campbeltown, where the rich aroma from the local distillery made the air quite intoxicating. One day I was coming up harbour in blinding rain and unfortunately mistook the channel and went hard aground. We got off within the hour as the tide rose and I went to my berth thinking nothing of it. Next morning I was peremptorily summoned to the office of the Naval Officer in Charge. He seemed upset about something. 'You ran your ship aground yesterday,' he spluttered. 'Why have you made no report of it? Why have you not rendered Form S 231, Details of Collision or Grounding?'

'Sir,' I protested. 'Submarines are designed to sit on the bottom.'

'Yes,' he said, 'But not fifty yards the wrong side of the channel buoy.'

I expressed deep sorrow and assured him that we were undamaged. But he was not mollified. 'Another thing, Wingfield. You have been here twenty-four hours and yet you have not called on me officially. Do submariners not observe the normal naval courtesies?'

I apologised profusely although I didn't think this tin-pot dictator rated a call anyway.

After a month or two of clockwork mouse we were ordered to Sheerness for a refit. Because of the tendency of all ships and aircraft to attack anything which looks like a U-boat, we were given a surface escort. Ours was a destroyer commanded by Ian Maitland-MacGill-Crichton – a Scot I would think. We were approaching E-boat alley – the searched channel along the Norfolk, Suffolk and Essex coast, as dusk fell. As was the custom I made what was a night intention signal. 'In the event of enemy attack I intend to remain on the surface.' Quick as a flash the destroyer replied, 'So do I!' In 1948 I offered this anecdote to the *Saturday Evening Post*, who published it in their column called 'The Perfect Squelch', and I received £250 for it. Since then it has been pirated by various naval authors; but it is true and it happened to me.

The trigger-happy attitude of the RAF and all our allied Air Forces was a constant worry to our submarines. *Spearfish* was a little late in returning from patrol one day in 1940 and was asked to report her Estimated Time of Arrival – the usual preliminary to posting a boat overdue. 'ETA noon tomorrow if the RAF will cease attacking me,' was the reply. I myself was attacked by Norwegian, French, American, Italian, Japanese and British aircraft. I expect some of the pilots are wearing decorations for sinking me as I always disappeared fast – to safety at a depth of 100 feet.

We had an encounter in the Thames Estuary with a Heinkel bomber on our way in to Sheerness. In an attempt to deter the RAF from attacking us we used to fly a large white ensign from our retractable mast. The Heinkel's intentions were clearly hostile so we dived to periscope depth, which should have ensured safety. Not so, however. The enemy went back and forth, peppering us with machine-gun fire. Presumably he had dropped his bombs so we were not in danger but the patter of bullets on the hull was irritating. He went away at last and we surfaced. It then dawned on us that the mast was still at full height and the Heinkel had been shooting at a white ensign trailing along just above the surface.

Back at Sheerness things were a bit quieter. No longer were we entertained by dogfights in the sky; no longer were the streets littered with cartridge clips. The Germans had given up daylight raids. The RAF had made them too costly. Night raids were to continue for years, with much of London being devastated. But what a lot survived. The Tower of London, St Paul's Cathedral, Buckingham Palace – none of them seriously damaged despite the raging infernos around them.

About Easter 1941 I was appointed to command HM Submarine *Umpire*, then in the course of construction at Chatham.

9

LOSS OF *UMPIRE* (MAY – JULY 1941)

W e rented a house in Maidstone Road from which I drove daily to the dockyard to watch the building and fitting out of *Umpire* and to learn something about her internal economy. The U-class were excellent little submarines, fairly slow, rather short-range and with a limited number of torpedoes, but exactly what was wanted in Malta. They did great execution against Rommel's supply lines but suffered rather heavy losses. However, these were quickly made up by new building. *Umpire* was bound for Malta after working up.

Wanklyn in *Upholder* was one of the early submarine aces. He had a magnificent record of sinking and seldom returned from patrol without a good score. But as often happens to the most successful, his flotilla commander could not bear to let him go when he was due for

HM Submarine Umpire

72

relief. He was kept on too long and perhaps acquired something of an invulnerability complex. His last patrol was brilliantly conducted but the escorts were on their toes. Once they had located *Upholder* on their sonar they hunted her relentlessly. Deeper and deeper she went, far beyond her test depth, but still the depth-charge bombardment continued. Eventually the enemy pings ceased to produce an echo. Only a circle of oil fuel marked the spot where her hull lay 1,000 fathoms down. His VC was well earned.[31]

Umpire was completed and I gave her the motto 'Keep on keeping on'. We sailed on 17 July 1941.

Around midnight on 19 July she was sunk off Great Yarmouth by a Royal Navy armed trawler called *Peter Hendrick*. She was rammed in the torpedo room and sank very quickly. One of the torpedo men gallantly closed the watertight door in the after end of the compartment which ensured that he and his mates all drowned, but gave a chance to the rest of the crew. The submarine settled on the bottom in about 70 feet of water. [32, *]

I had been on the bridge with the officer of the watch and two lookouts. We floated off as the ship went down but not before I had time to shout to the trawler, 'You bastard! You've sunk a British submarine.' I was wearing a special kapok-lined Burberry which my wife had given me as a present. I only wore it this one time but it saved my life. I didn't even get my cap wet as the ship sank. I remember my binoculars floating in front of me, chin high. The officer of the watch, Sub-Lieutenant Godden, and the two lookouts, all of whom were wearing heavy leather seaboots, floated near me and even held on to me for a time, but one by one they dropped away. I continued to float, held up by the buoyancy of my Burberry. I remember nothing much more except the quiet conviction that I was drowning. It wasn't even painful – just a quiet drifting into unconsciousness. There seemed to

---

* According to Hezlet's *History of British Submarine Operations in the Second World War*: On 19 July the new submarine *Umpire*, on passage with convoy EC4 off the Wash, broke down and dropped astern. She was rammed and sunk by an escort of convoy FS44 coming the other way. Wingfield and fourteen men were rescued but two other officers and fourteen men were drowned.

be nothing difficult about dying. My past did *not* all come before me. It was all rather prosaic.

However, at what must have been the eleventh hour – actually forty minutes after the sinking, I felt a wooden oar near me and clutched it desperately. The whaler's crew from the *Peter Hendrick* had chanced upon my almost lifeless body in the dark and swirling tide. They hauled me aboard, put me face down in the bottom of the boat and deposited me on the trawler's deck. The first thing I remember was someone reading out from the gold bracelet which I wore on my wrist 'MRG Wingfield, HM Submarines'.

'At least we've got the bugger's name,' said one of my rescuers. I protested that I wasn't dead and asked if there were any other survivors.

'None so far,' they said.

'I'm the captain,' I said. 'You'd better throw me back.'

However, they took me to the ratings' mess and gave me some rum and I was soon OK. The trawler captain came down to the ratings' mess in a very hostile frame of mind. 'It was entirely your fault,' he said, and stumped off. The men looked after me well but it seemed odd not to be accommodated in the wardroom. It was as if they thought I was a German.

I was landed eventually at Yarmouth and given some dry uniform. Later I sent some money for the trawler crew addressed c/o the Commanding Officer, Royal Naval Reserve. I never had an acknowledgement.

Some hours later about twenty of the crew escaped from the stricken *Umpire* using the Davis Submarine Escape Apparatus. First Lieutenant Edward Young and one other came up through the conning tower hatch without using this apparatus. Edward Young described the experience in his book *One of Our Submarines*.[33]

All these were picked up by the surface ships which had congregated at the scene of the accident. About ten men failed to escape and the other three who had been on the bridge with me drowned. There were also several civilian dockyard men on board who were not trained in the use of the escape apparatus and, sadly, none of them survived.

It is painful for me to recall this unfortunate affair, but I will try to give a factual account of the events leading up to the collision. *Umpire* was on her way north, escorted by some sort of a motor launch whose purpose was to ward off medal-hungry attackers. We were supposed to be with the north-bound convoy but due to engine trouble we had dropped astern and were on our own. Our so-called escort steamed off into the night and we never saw her again. At the subsequent inquiry her CO insisted it was my job to keep station on him. The reverse was true.

We were now on the extreme western side of the searched channel with little space between us and the coastal minefields to port. Suddenly the southbound convoy appeared, twenty or thirty dimly lit merchant ships escorted by armed trawlers on each flank. My navigation lights were on but dimmed in view of the likelihood of E-boat attack. I saw the lights of the *Peter Hendrick* dead ahead and turned 20° to port, contrary to the Rules of the Road. Had I turned to starboard, the correct action, I would have put myself right across the bows of the column of southbound ships.

The *Peter Hendrick* turned to starboard and rammed me, possibly thinking I was a U-boat or possibly, as their captain later insisted, because I had not obeyed the Rules of the Road. As I have explained, it was impossible for me to do this owing to the stream of southbound ships close to starboard.

An inquiry was held at Chatham which reached some rather wishy-washy conclusions, attaching no blame to anyone, not even my useless escort. They did not recommend that I be court-martialled (as is normal after the loss of an HM ship), owing to the number of witnesses from different ships who would have to be called and the disruption this would cause to the east-coast convoy system. I was sorry not to have had an opportunity to clear my name, but as I was appointed to a new command soon after the sinking, I take that as sufficient vindication.

With hindsight, I can see I made two mistakes. E-boats were German motor torpedo boats. At this time they were raiding our Channel and North Sea convoy routes nightly, escaping at high speed. Our own

Motor Torpedo Boats (MTBs) were no match for them, despite the gallant exploits of Peter Scott and others. I should have switched on my navigation lights to full brightness as soon as I saw the approaching convoy, disregarding the E-boat threat. Secondly, in turning to port I should have made a bold turn, say 90°, and disregarded the minefield danger. It turned out that the declared minefield was not, as I had thought, a continuous line of mines but a few widely spread clusters.

It would have been reasonable for the *Peter Hendrick* to have held her course or even turned closer to the convoy, which would have left us well clear. Her turn to starboard made a collision certain.

10

HM SUBMARINE *STURGEON* (1941–42)

I spent my survivor's leave at Lynchmere House, building a hen-house. I wrote a letter of thanks to the makers of my life-saving Burberry, which they much appreciated. They told me that despite the number of lives saved by their product they had been arbitrarily closed down by the Ministry of Supply as non-essential to the war effort. I visited some of the next-of-kin of those members of the *Umpire* who lost their lives. Some were grateful, some resentful, but one buxom lady was quite down-to-earth. 'What's my pension then?' she asked.

Back at Fort Blockhouse with some nominal duties in the Spare Submarine Crew, I realised I was under observation to see if I had suffered any ill effects from my experience. I was sure I had not and I looked forward to getting another submarine command.

About this time the commander-in-chief Portsmouth issued an order to all naval shore establishments to run down their stocks of wine. It was unsuitable, he said, in these days of rationing and austerity that officers' messes should have thousands of pounds worth of vintage wines in their cellars. To implement this policy (an idiotic one in my opinion), Fort Blockhouse reduced the price of all its stock to three or four shillings a bottle. As an old and well-run mess it had a large cellar, much of it maturing for use in later years, but everything had to go. A friend called Alan Baker and I loyally devoted ourselves to this duty and nightly ploughed our way through Nuits-St-George, Macon, Chianti and Heidsieck.

Mention of the Blockhouse wardroom reminds me of a story from the early weeks of the war. One of the elderly L-boats was overdue and was eventually judged to have been sunk by enemy action. The wardroom mess secretary promptly sent off the captain's outstanding mess bill to the widow with a request for payment. Unfortunately this arrived before the official notification of her husband's death, which caused something of a rumpus. A mess meeting was called at which the Mess Committee were likened to Shylock. Eventually it was agreed that the mess would not press for payment of mess bills from next-of-kin. This, of course, resulted in the active submariners ensuring that their indebtedness to the mess was always at a high level.

STURGEON AND NORTH RUSSIA
(AUGUST 1941 – SPRING 1942)

After an idle but happy couple of months I was appointed in command of HM Submarine *Sturgeon*. This was one of the earlier S-class submarines which had achieved some fame under David Gregory's command during the Norwegian campaign. *Sturgeon* was a cranky boat and had a dangerous habit of breaking surface when a full salvo of six torpedoes was fired. This was clearly a fault in design but the Royal Corps of Naval Construction would never admit it. We were always told it was due to bad handling of the submarine by the crew. It certainly made life dangerous for us.

One of my particular complaints against the naval constructors, who are a para-naval organisation who put on uniform when it suits them, is that our ships often seem to be inferior materially to those of our allies and enemies. Is it possible that the best naval architects join the top shipbuilders, the less good join minor firms and those whom nobody will employ commercially become naval constructors? One case in point is the design of submarine periscopes. In the early days of submarines the gyro compass had not been invented so there was only a magnetic compass (known to us as Faithful Freddie) to depend on. In order to avoid magnetic deviation all the conning tower and the periscopes were made of brass, which is non-magnetic. Fifty years later when the Sperry gyro compass was universally fitted and most reliable, Faithful Freddie was still installed in the conning tower and our periscopes were still made of brass. This had an enormous effect on our tactics. A brass periscope, due to the weakness of the material, can only have 15 feet of unsupported length when fully raised. Since most convoy escorts drew 16 or 17 feet, it was not possible to pass under an escort by lowering the periscope. He would knock off your periscope standard if he passed over. It was thus necessary to go deep – and blind, to pass inside the screen. The Germans and all our allies had steel periscopes with an unsupported length of 18 to 19 feet or more. When they wanted to penetrate the escort screen all they had to do was lower the periscope and the destroyer, frigate or corvette passed harmlessly overhead.

Captain at the periscope: Wingfield (crouched) in HM Submarine Sturgeon

Nevertheless, I was pleased to get command of *Sturgeon* which I held for nearly a year. We operated on the coast of Norway from a base in North Russia called Polyarnoe, near Murmansk. The climate was appalling, with sub-zero temperatures and strong gales. Sometimes

HMS Sturgeon *returning damaged from off Narvik, unable to dive, September 1942*

after a night on the surface charging batteries, the gun on the fore-deck would be just a mound of ice. Of course it soon melted when we dived. The sea in the area does not freeze, thanks to the Gulf Stream, which makes Murmansk an ice-free port. It was here that most of the massive aid we gave Russia (for which we received little thanks) was unloaded. The dockers were mostly women and their working lives must have been short. They wore odd bits of sacking round their shoulders and wrapped their feet in cloths. Few had boots. Nobody of course lived in North Russia from choice. The workers were employed on a forced-labour basis as in Siberia, while the management were rewarded with high salaries.

We had an interpreter called Bella who had taken a degree at Birmingham University. She took a great fancy to my wristwatch, this being an unobtainable item at that time. She kept raising her offer until eventually I told her it was far too high. 'What does it matter? I have plenty of roubles but there is nothing to spend them on up here.'

There were few pleasant features in life at Polyarnoe but I remember Christmas Day 1941. The postman came round on a sleigh drawn by two magnificently antlered reindeer. It somewhat distracts from the impact of the anecdote if I admit that he did this every day – reindeer sleighs were the normal means of transport.

On my birthday, 16 January 1942, we were surprised to be invited by the Russians to a skiing expedition. They normally avoided contact with us but this was a special day as we were going to see the sun rise for the first time in two months. Accordingly we strapped on our skis, courtesy of Lord Nuffield's Fund for the Services, and tramped up a small mountain near the base. My first lieutenant, Hugh Brunner, unlike me was an excellent skier. He dazzled the Russians with his Christies and slaloms. Our allies had short, rather narrow, military skis which were good for rough cross-country work but no fun to use. Apparently the Finnish army, which was largely ski-borne, had been running rings round the foot-slogging Red Army. The orders came from Moscow to raise a ski regiment but who was to teach this bourgeois activity? Eventually an elderly officer was brought out of retirement and became the chief instructor. He spoke quite good English and had been to Switzerland in Tsarist days. Somehow he must have escaped the purge of the Imperial Army officers

But to return to our mountain. We reached the top, consulted our watches and sure enough the red rim of the sun rose a degree or so above the horizon before disappearing again. 'Hurrah! Spring is here,' we all said as we started down the hillside. We invited our six Red Navy officers to join us for vodka in our mess. They accepted with pleasure but when they arrived it was a set of six entirely different officers, none of whom had been on our expedition. Other people who have had dealings with these suspicious characters have had similar experiences.

I don't know what the temperature fell to, but one night a group of sailors were returning from the canteen. One of them felt tired and said he would rest for a while. Apparently he fell asleep. He was found in the morning, frozen stiff.

One of our cruisers, *Trinidad* I think, was sunk not far out at sea from our base. There were hundreds of men in the water and it was essential to rescue them quickly. We appealed to the Russian admiral to send out one of his destroyers to pick up survivors but he said it was impossible as it was a public holiday and the ships must stay in port.[34]

There were half a dozen large K-class Russian submarines at our base. Technically they were first class but it seemed to us they had little idea of the strategic and tactical uses of submarines. We asked them why they seldom went to sea. 'No use going out if there are no targets,' they said. But one of them did venture out when the German battleship *Tirpitz* was reported. A few days later he returned firing his gun and blowing his siren as he came up the fjord. He claimed to have seriously damaged, perhaps sunk, the *Tirpitz*. He was immediately made a Hero of the Soviet Union which, among other benefits, entitles the holder to free rides on the Moscow trams for life.

We were extremely sceptical of the claim. It seems he had fired two torpedoes on a 170° track (i.e. almost directly astern), and had distinctly heard two hits. Given that the *Tirpitz* usually cruised at nearly 30 knots and the speed of the Russian torpedoes was 40 knots, a hit was almost impossible. The two bangs were probably the torpedoes exploding on hitting the bottom. German records after the war made no mention of this attack. *Tirpitz* probably did not know she had been fired at.

Targets were few around North Cape, but I sank a 2,500 ton ship off one of the fjords further south. It was a satisfying attack as I hit with two torpedoes and the target slowly tipped bows down and disappeared with the propeller still turning.

On another patrol I was ordered to a position right up Trondheim Fjord. A big target was apparently expected. The trouble was the fjord was mined. We assumed that the mines were laid so as to catch surface ships so we went in at 100 feet depth. This worked quite well although the scraping of the mooring wires along our hull concentrated our minds a bit. We sank a medium-sized merchant ship but saw no major war vessels. On our return the minefield was again traversed at 100 feet and we finally surfaced a few miles offshore after a 22-hour dive. The battery was quite exhausted and the air so foul that a cigarette would not burn.*

I was sent for by Admiral Sir Max Horton after the patrol to describe my activities. He was rather non-committal and asked to see my charts of the patrol. These included appropriate fixes at 15-minute

---

*   Hezlet: On 7th June *Sturgeon* and *Minerve* (Lieutenant de Vaisseau P Sonneville), on their way home, were diverted to the south west of the Lofotens to try to intercept a German squadron. When the enemy passed to the inside of the Lofotens, Wingfield in *Sturgeon* was ordered to an inshore patrol off Trondheim, having to pass through a known German minefield to get there. He had withdrawn to seawards to charge batteries when the German cruiser *Lutzow* passed.

intervals. It appears that he was satisfied and much to my surprise and delight I was awarded the Distinguished Service Order on 17 November 1942, 'in the Sixth Year of our Reign' as the citation says.[35]

On another patrol I was placed as senior submarine commander at the centre of a ring of submarines placed outside Alten Fjord where the *Tirpitz* was based. It was believed that she was about to sail and it seemed certain that I would be right in her path. I would of course have made my attack, we would of course have broken surface, and I would of course have been sunk very quickly by the escort of six Maas-class destroyers. I would, of course, have received a posthumous VC.*

But things worked out differently. The elderly *Sturgeon* suddenly became non-operational due to the fracture of the bell-crank lever operating the after hydroplanes. The planes were in fact flapping. When we were bow down they went hard-a-dive. When bow up, they went hard-a-rise. There was no possible repair we could make so I radioed for permission to leave patrol. A couple of RAF Beauforts [twin-engined torpedo-bombers] escorted us on the surface to Lerwick in the Shetlands and thence to a repair yard. The *Tirpitz* steamed happily through the gap I had left and wreaked havoc on some unfortunate convoy.[36]

We were ordered to Iceland soon after this in order to assist in the protection of convoy PQ17. The idea was that *Sturgeon* and another S-class submarine would be stationed in the centre of the convoy ready to attack the *Tirpitz* should she appear. **

To my relief she left us alone, although after we had left the convoy it was almost completely destroyed by U-boats and air attack. Admiral Pound, First Sea Lord, had never fought a sea battle. Unhappily he decided the passage of PQ17 gave him a last chance. From his desk in Whitehall he virtually took tactical command of the escorting forces over the heads of the men on the spot. It was he who gave the disastrous

---

* Hezlet: In August, after Lutzow had again slipped by, *Sturgeon* sank the *Bolten Hagen* of 3335 tons with three torpedoes fired at 1600 yards. Though counter attacked by the escort, and depth-charged, Wingfield escaped undamaged.

** Hezlet: *Sturgeon* was sent as close escort for PQ15. Consisting of 25 ships, one of the largest Arctic convoys of the war, after which on 30 April she took up an offshore patrol position.

order to scatter which ensured the loss of almost every ship and caused the Merchant Navy to feel betrayed by the RN.*

Nothing very interesting happened to us. We seemed to spend a lot of time in fog. One day when it was clear, we observed a German reconnaissance plane circling the fleet. All day it went round and round clockwise. One escort boat got bored and flashed the aircraft, 'Please go the other way. I'm getting giddy.' Believe it or not the aircraft flashed an acknowledgement and promptly commenced circling anti-clockwise.

We had one good laugh. A U-boat torpedoed a ship not far from us. She started to sink and the crew lowered the lifeboats. The crew of the next ship in the line thought *they* had been hit and frantically started scrambling into their boats. When they discovered that they were quite undamaged they hoisted their boats again in some embarrassment.

ST NAZAIRE (EARLY 1942 – AUGUST 1942)

We had a couple of interesting assignments in the spring of 1942. The first was in the Clyde where we trained the party of Royal Marines, led by Colonel Hasler, for the raid up the Gironde Estuary. This involved loading their collapsible canoes into the submarine, diving, surfacing, assembling the two-man canoes and paddling off.

Another submarine did the actual operation, which was very successful in that half a dozen merchant ships in Bordeaux harbour were sunk by explosive charges fixed to the hulls by the 'cockleshell heroes'. Sadly, only two of the ten raiders, 'Blondie' Hasler and his partner Marine Sparks, got away through the German net, returning to Britain via Spain.[37]

In March we were ordered to Plymouth to prepare for a highly secret operation which turned out to be the raid on St Nazaire. Our job was to act as a navigational marker just off the port and to guide the raiding force into the entrance channel.**

---

* Hezlet: The weight of the German attack on Convoy PQ17 fell in early July, but *Sturgeon* had already been withdrawn on 2/3 July because she was short of fuel.

** Hezlet: In March *Sturgeon* was sent south to co-operate with the raid on St Nazaire, took part in preliminary exercises off Plymouth, and sailed on 23 March to act as a navigational beacon, and returned to the Clyde on 29th.

There was a conference before we sailed at which all the details of the assault plan were revealed. The object of the raid was to destroy the large dry dock in the naval base which was the only dock on that coast of France which could take the major German ships like *Scharnhorst* and *Bismarck*. An old ex-US Navy destroyer named *Campbeltown*, packed with explosives, was to steam full speed towards the lock gates, force its way into the dock then blow itself up by time fuses. Meanwhile the army commandos would be blowing up the rest of the dockyard cranes, boiler houses, everything.

I listened to all this with intense interest. Several of the senior officers asked questions but the chap sitting beside me said nothing and appeared slightly bored. I asked him what his job was in the raid. 'I'm the Naval Force Commander,' replied Captain 'Red' Ryder, who was to earn a well-merited VC.

We sailed two days early and reached our position off the entrance channel without difficulty. Accuracy was essential so we fixed our position by frequent periscope bearings of lighthouses, churches, etc. on shore until we knew we were within 50 yards of our appointed station. The only slight worry was the large number of fishing vessels in the area. We didn't want to get entangled in their nets or to let them sight our periscope.

Before dawn on 28 March 1942 we surfaced and showed a green light to seaward. The raiding force, consisting of *Campbeltown*, eighteen motor launches or MTBs escorted by destroyers, soon came in sight and passed on each side of us. To my alarm, Robin Jenks, commanding the Hunt-class destroyer *Atherstone*, turned on his loudhailer and greeted me: 'Good morning, Mervyn. Many thanks.' Every fisherman in the area must have been alerted but amazingly the enemy remained quiet. The force had encountered enemy light forces on the way over from Plymouth but the defenders of St Nazaire were taken by surprise. Not until the final stages of the approach did the Germans react, when they opened fierce fire from all their batteries and did much damage to our ships. But by this time I was on my way home. We heard the distant noise of the battle and were glad to be out of it.

The raid was a success. The dock was unusable for the rest of the war, but the price was high. Of the 630 soldiers and sailors involved, 144 were killed, 215 became POWs and 271 returned to England.[38]

As a postscript I might add a story one of the doctors at Plymouth told me. After the raid there were plenty of wounded to deal with, but one soldier reported sick with a tiresome complaint which could only have been acquired on shore.

'How on earth did you pick this up?' queried the doctor. 'You have been sealed in your landing ship for ten days.'

'Well, it was like this, Sir,' the soldier answered. 'My only job at St Nazaire was to blow up a crane and when I'd done this I had to wait on the dock for a motor launch to pick me up. This French girl comes along and says, "Hello Tommy, would you like a nice time?" and that, Sir, is how it must have happened.'

Meanwhile a fierce battle raged all around him.

In the Kaiser's War, the Raid on Zeebrugge brought much fame to Admiral Keyes. The losses were also heavy – 195 out of 1,800, but unfortunately all in vain. The object was to bottle up the U-boats but they found an alternative route in a few days which avoided the blockships, and thus suffered little inconvenience.

I am always surprised that the Germans did not once mount a raid against England. There were plenty of suitable targets and they had seen many of our raids achieving striking success, such as at Bruneval, where we captured the new German radar. Perhaps the German military mind is too rigid and does not approve of side-shows run by private armies. To some extent they are probably right. In the Middle East private armies and navies, and even air forces (such as the SAS), proliferated but I doubt if they did much good. However, they were immensely enjoyable for the participants and made good reading in the newspapers when victories were few and far between.

In autumn 1942 I turned over *Sturgeon* to the dockyard for refit and was appointed to HM Submarine *Taurus* under construction by Vickers at Barrow-in-Furness.[39] The T-class were modern design, medium size (1,500 tons), ocean-going submarines. The early boats had already had many successes. I looked forward with pleasure to my new command.

11

TAKING COMMAND OF *TAURUS* (1942–43)

L ancashire, in that time of austerity, was a pretty dreary sort of place. However, the shipyard was a hive of activity with several submarines in various stages of construction. My engineer officer was already there and had made himself familiar with all the complexities of this latest example of submarine design. Vickers were no strangers to underwater craft, having built *Holland I* (now in the submarine museum after seventy years on the sea bed) and many hundreds more. I believe they passed the 1000 mark not long ago.

The managing director told me one day at lunch how Vickers had built two identical aircraft carriers for the Admiralty. The Countess of X, who launched the first one, was presented with a diamond brooch to mark the occasion as was, and still is, the custom. The Countess of Y was asked to launch the second one, which presented a problem to Sir John. The ladies were known to be good friends so the brooch for Lady Y must be every bit as good as Lady X's. Sir John consulted the jeweller, who assured him there was no difficulty. 'I can give you not only a similar brooch, but exactly the same one. Lady X sold it back to us shortly after the launch for £1,000.'

My wife Sheila was asked to launch a U-class submarine for the Polish Navy. Very foolishly I declined on the grounds that with a baby due in a few weeks she was not in good shape for a public ceremony. I assumed the invitation would be renewed after Richard was born on 30 December. Not so. 'You had your chance and turned it down,' they told me. So no sparkling souvenir of Barrow-in-Furness adorns her jewel case.

Crew of Taurus, *1944*

I had always thought that the standard naval officer's uniform in superfine cloth with silver-gilt stripes of rank was unsuitable for submariners. So while at Barrow I had a local tailor make me a suit of battle-dress in ordinary navy serge. It was exactly the same as the army pattern, only blue with stripes in yellow cloth on the shoulders. People thought this rather daring at the time but it wasn't long before the Admiralty caught on and made it official, thus saving everyone a lot of money.

Vickers did their usual splendid job and delivered the submarine on time and in sparkling order. Contractor's sea trials, including the first dive, were successful. The final stage was for me to sign a receipt. 'Received T-class submarine P339. Price paid £337,000', and excellent value she was.

Taurus had a 4-inch gun just like *Odin's*. I soon had the gun's crew working out the drill for quick surfacing and opening fire, and we developed quite a high speed. Forty years later one of the gun's crew told me they got rather tired of being compared disparagingly with *Odin's* winning crew. Going up Loch Long one day to the torpedo firing range I saw a ruined cottage on the shore. 'Gun action!' I ordered. 'Put six rounds into that building to port.' This was done with great precision and much enjoyed by the gun's crew. I thought nothing of it until some days later when a letter was received from the Duke of Argyll complaining that one of his foresters had been put in fear of his life and a valuable wood-store destroyed. My squadron commander said, 'Wingfield, you really must not do this sort of thing.' Like many another submarine captain I was, at this time, beginning to get a little too big for my boots. After all, we had a high scarcity value and could get away with almost anything.

We spent most of January 1943 working up in the Clyde area, a boring but necessary procedure, before sailing on a shake-down patrol to the North Cape. It was rough and cold and totally uneventful. Everything went well and the officers and crew settled down, if not as one happy family, at least amicably.

I think it was on this patrol that we were given some experimental food for trial. As is well known, you can't tell cooks anything and they don't read directions. Our chef took the sack of dehydrated spinach, and tipped the whole lot into his largest saucepan. As he brought it to the boil the spinach swelled and swelled, all over the cooker and on to the deck. The green slime even started advancing up the passage towards the control room before being checked. On the empty sack it was possible to read the inscription 'Ration for 600 men'.

The BBC invited me to London after this patrol to record a piece for a programme called *War Report* on the Home Service. I enjoyed this experience and occasionally play the 78rpm record which starts 'This is Lieutenant Commander Wingfield who …'

TAURUS IN THE MEDITERRANEAN (SEPTEMBER 1942 – SPRING 1943)

After a few days' leave during which I bought a small house called Farthings in Headley Road, Liphook, and also a car (a Standard 9 to replace the Wolseley which I had sold earlier), we sailed for Gibraltar. Although the petrol ration for the public was zero gallons per month, submariners got a small allowance. We ran a car throughout the war and for about a year Sheila transported Admiral Vian's children to school – for which we received remarkably little thanks. It was said of Admiral Vian that he had no manners but if he had had any they would have been bad. But he did tell a story against himself about two sailors painting the ship's side outside his cabin. Through the open porthole he overheard the following conversation:

'Do you know what day this is, Bert?'

'No, Bill. What day is it?'

'It's our Admiral's birthday, Bert, that's what it is. Forty-nine years ago today *The Times* newspaper had an announcement "To Mr and Mrs Vian, the gift of a son, Philip." Christ, what a gift!'[40]

There was a small submarine officers' mess at Gibraltar where we spent a few days. It had one admirable feature – sherry and port were free. Two decanters stood on the sideboard from which one helped oneself. I suppose we paid for it in our mess subscription but it was certainly cheap and the arrangement saved all the bother of wine bills.

Later in the war a young submarine commander called John Fyfe overdid the sherry a bit and thought he would play a practical joke on a rather pompous destroyer captain whose ship was berthed astern of Fyfe's submarine. Silently he let go all the destroyer's mooring ropes, then went on board his submarine and started the electric motors slow ahead. The screws turned and the wash quietly pushed the destroyer towards the middle of the harbour. Not even the gangway falling off the dockside woke up the quartermaster on watch. It was quite a time before the situation revealed itself to the infuriated captain, who quite failed to see the funny side.[41]

Lt Cdr Wingfield with Submarine Squadron Captain Barney Fawkes,
returning to Algiers after a successful patrol, March 1943

Our first operational base for *Taurus* was Algiers, where there was a large operational flotilla based on the depot ship *Maidstone*, commanded by Captain Barney Fawkes.[42] There was also a fleet of battleships, many cruisers and uncounted smaller craft. Occasionally there were air raids by the Italians but they were half-hearted affairs. Our barrage of anti-aircraft fire was terrific and coupled with a smokescreen put up by the army it deterred most of the Italian pilots.

One night I was dining in the famous cruiser *Aurora* with a Royal Marine friend called Brickwood – son of the Portsmouth brewer.[43] When the sirens went off he took me up to his battle-station, the secondary armament control top. There we had a superb view of the fireworks. I even saw *Taurus* making her contribution with the Oerlikon gun. During a raid on another night when I was ashore I even saw an American colonel firing his pistol into the air.

The Aletti Hotel was a popular resort of both the Army and Navy.[44] The Germans had apparently decamped with all the wine glasses so we drank our wine out of sawn-off beer bottles and jolly good it was too. I became quite friendly with a captain in the Intelligence Corps who was originally Oliver Baldwin, but when his father Stanley took a peerage he became Viscount Corvedale.[45] He had a jeep and we made several interesting expeditions to ancient sites including a Roman port. The docks, complete with stone mooring bollards, were in good order after 2,000 years. Oliver was furious with the US Army. He owned a villa on the coast near Algiers and naturally thought he might be given it as a billet. But no, the villa was allocated to two US Army colonels and he was given a room at the Aletti.

Another evening we had a ladies' guest night in *Maidstone*. One of the guests was an extremely good-looking Irish-American girl called Kay Summersby. Her primary duty was as General Eisenhower's chauffeur but she was generally believed to solace his loneliness to the best of her ability. (In her book she more or less admits that she was his mistress for two years.) Kay had borrowed the general's car to come to the party and when an air raid started she was pretty worried, mostly on account of the risk of the Cadillac being hit. In the end she had to stay the night on board in a spare cabin. As it says on Madame de Pompadour's tombstone, 'On dort seul, enfin.'

I remember walking the quarterdeck of *Maidstone* with Ben Bryant, the much decorated commanding officer of *Safari*. He was older than me and had had brilliant successes in the North Sea and later in the Mediterranean. We had lost one submarine the previous week and we were scanning the horizon for another which was overdue. He dismissed all losses as due to incompetence and insisted that we peacetime-trained submariners would not lose our lives by trying to do stupid things. But there was one submarine commander who had gone into a defended harbour and been sunk by gunfire from shore batteries. The word went around that he had been in the habit of using Benzedrine as a stimulant.

PATROLS FROM ALGIERS (MARCH – JUNE 1943)

My crew were looking a bit down in the mouth before we sailed for our first Mediterranean patrol. We had lost three submarines in the previous few weeks but we still had about ten left. I remember making a pompous speech to the crew somewhat on these lines: 'We are about to sail on our first real war patrol. Our station will be off Toulon where we are to impose a blockade on the port. The French fleet is now under German control and it is our job to stop them getting out, also to stop any supplies getting in. Our immediate predecessor in this duty was Lord Nelson in 1803. We have had losses but not half as many as the Guards' Brigade at Kasserine and that hasn't stopped them continuing to fight. So shall we. In any case we have no choice. Don't worry. We are a well-trained crew; we have a fine ship and I am a most cautious CO. I feel sure we shall have a successful patrol.'

On the way to our area we went up the Spanish coast where we encountered a Spanish ship of about 3,000 tons and sank it by gunfire after a long chase. We picked up three survivors from a raft, the captain and two seamen. I made the captain, who spoke good English, comfortable in the wardroom but he was most objectionable, saying we were worse than German U-boats. I told him we had declared a blockade of all French ports and if he chose to be a blockade-runner he must take the consequences. I got tired of him after twenty-four hours and went into the port of Almeria where I handed him and his crew over to the Spanish police who met us at the harbour. As Spain was neutral our arrival caused quite a sensation.*

---

* Hezlet: On 6 March, on his first Mediterranean patrol in *Taurus*, Wingfield had already sunk a small sailing vessel off Cape Ferrat, when off Merseilles he met the 3118 ton Spanish *Bartolo* which was on charter to the Germans. He fired four torpedoes at a range of 3000 yards but one torpedo ran under and the others missed. Two hours later two more torpedoes were fired at 500 yards, and one hit and sank *Bartolo*. Four days later he sank the 1770 ton Italian *Derna*, firing three torpedos at 1500 yards hitting with one. Finally he sank a tug and lighter by gunfire.

On return from this patrol the commander-in-chief, Admiral Cunningham, sent for me and asked if I thought I was right to sink a ship with a cargo of oranges. I explained how I interpreted the rules of closed blockade, to which he replied, rather indecisively, 'Yes, I suppose so. But the neutrals are making an awful row about it.' After a limp handshake, I departed. This was the only time I met this famous figure. I think it must have been one of his off days.

This incident concluded with a letter from the British Consul, Barcelona, thanking me for doing a useful job. 'Since you sank the *Bartolo* all trade with occupied France has ceased. Well done,' he wrote.

We had a few more patrols from Algiers. On one of them I went along the coast to Monaco where I saw a beautiful white steam yacht which I could easily have sunk. But no, I held back. Would it advance the war effort? Obviously not. So I refrained from shooting a sitter which would have put my tonnage aggregate up to 1,000 tons. (We all kept our scores carefully.) Then I saw the Casino. If I shelled it, surely I would rate a headline: 'Wingfield, the Man who Broke the Bank at Monte Carlo'. It was tempting but I decided against it, much to the chagrin of my gun's crew.

Back at Algiers I was relating this story to some friends in the wardroom, one of whom, Alastair Mars, was most interested in what I said. Next day he sailed, went straight to Monte Carlo and shelled the Casino with his gun. He wrote this up pretty well in his patrol report and the *Daily Mirror* came out with the headline: 'The Man who Broke the Bank at Monte Carlo'.[46]

In Malta some time later, *Taurus* was alongside Alastair Mars' submarine *Unbroken* when a petty officer came over and asked to speak to me. He seemed to want to transfer from *Unbroken* to *Taurus* because he thought his captain was half-mad and dangerous. I told him I could not take him on and he must make the best of it. 'It's a dangerous war,' I said. *Unbroken* survived, Mars added a bar to his DSC for sinking a cruiser and faded out of my ken for some time. His relationship with the Admiralty deteriorated later, however, and he was to sue them for wrongful dismissal.

Our last patrol from Algiers took us to the Tyrrhenian Sea – an unpopular area owing to the clearness of the water which made it easy for aircraft to pick up submerged submarines. It was also within range of the many airfields of the west coast of Italy. We had no trouble, however, perhaps because we kept a very good lookout and always sighted hostile aircraft in time to dive.

It is remarkable how one's eyesight improves when life depends on it. The ratings acting as lookouts did not often make the first sighting. Usually it was the officer of the watch. But the keenest sight belonged to the captain, due to his longer experience and intense concentration. It may seem surprising but the ability to pick up very distant objects improves with practice whether by day or by night. Unlike the previous generation of submarines we were lucky to have a binocular periscope which saved a lot of eye strain.

Somewhere off Elba we sank a Portuguese blockade-runner of about 1,500 tons by gunfire.* There was a row about this one too, as of course Portugal was neutral, but it seems I was supported by my superiors. We also sank a three-masted sailing ship, rather to my regret. I fired one torpedo which missed ahead as she was only making about 3 knots. The next one hit and she blew up with a spectacular display of fireworks. She must have been carrying ammunition. Being so near the enemy coast it was not possible to pick up survivors.**

Our next base was Beirut in the Lebanon, a delightful port known in those days as the Paris of the Middle East. We were accommodated in the former French Foreign Legion barracks, and very comfortable they were for us officers, but less so for our ship's company, who were housed in converted stables.

---

*   Hezlet: On 13 April 1943 Wingfield sank the 520 ton Portuguese *Santa Irene* with gunfire about 30 nautical miles south-east of Bastia, Corsica.

**   Hezlet: In April Wingfield patrolled the Tyrrhenian Sea. On 5th, off Naples, a convoy passed out of range and on 7th she chased a target but was forced to dive by aircraft. On 14th she attacked a tanker, *Alcione C* of 521 tons by gunfire off Cape Alistio. After nineteen hits she fired two torpedoes at 500 and 750 yards one of which hit and sank her. On surfacing for the night she sighted a destroyer lying stopped and she had to dive again but was not detected. On 15th at night she fired two torpedoes at 600 and 800 yards range and sank the 443 ton four masted vessel, *Luigi*, who blew spectacularly.

Life was good in Beirut then. You could swim in the Mediterranean in the morning and ski at Aley in the afternoon. There were superb restaurants untroubled by food shortages and a busy nightlife centred on the Hotel St George. One night I met a genuine Circassian princess there – at least she said she was. I could see what made the girls of this race so much in demand for harems. Then there was a charming Greek girl cut off from her homeland for years. 'You are sailing tomorrow for Greece,' she said (surprising the information you can pick up in bars). 'Please, please bring me back just one little piece of Greece.' I promised faithfully to do this but alas I forgot. When I got back to Beirut there she was in the St George bar with hands outstretched. 'You have it?' she asked. 'Of course,' I said after a moment's hesitation, 'I'll go and get it for you.' I went down to the hotel beach and picked up a small stone. Her gratitude was overwhelming. 'I knew you wouldn't let me down,' she said.

We did several clandestine operations in Eastern Mediterranean waters, landing spies, agents or reconnaissance parties and picking up escapees. These were considered a waste of time by some of my colleagues, who were longing to get at the enemy. I rather enjoyed them. They were perfectly safe and always successful. The spies were delighted to be landed dry-shod at the right place, instead of being bundled out of an old bomber and parachuting down into the unknown, thinking of church spires. We landed one man on the island of Euboia, where he was to perform some activity against the enemy which involved a large bribe. For this purpose he had a bag which was rather heavy, containing as it did 500 gold sovereigns, which were then the most acceptable currency in Greece. We wished him luck and promised to be back at the same place in fourteen days. We made the rendezvous but he did not. In vain we flashed our recognition signals. Two weeks later we again waited for him off the beach, but once again we were unsuccessful. 'Poor Mr Aristides,' we said, 'he must have been caught by the Gestapo and probably tortured to death.' After the war when I was in the Admiralty I went down to the Naval Intelligence Department and enquired what had happened to the poor man. 'It's rather embarrassing,' I was told. 'It seems Aristides bought a farm with the gold sovereigns and spent the rest of the war supplying the Germans with fresh vegetables.'[47]

12

EASTERN MEDITERRANEAN
(JULY – AUGUST 1943)

The invasion of the Dodecanese was a ghastly failure and one of several for which Churchill must bear responsibility. The original plan was to capture Rhodes and then use its airfields to provide air cover for the capture of the other islands, Leros, Samos, Kos, and so on.

I landed a reconnaissance party on Rhodes including Colonel Sterling and a kilted officer called Major Dunbabin,* who reported that the island had been reinforced by a second division of German troops and that capture by our slender forces was not now possible.[48] General Maitland Wilson reported this to London, recommending that the operation be abandoned.[49] Churchill was furious and insisted that the invasion must proceed even without the essential air cover. Our troops were landed and immediately pinned down by the enemy air forces. The Navy did its best to support the Army, losing several destroyers and two submarines in the process. We even sent a submarine with field guns strapped to her deck but she didn't make it. I did one trip to Leros where the Durham Light Infantry were fighting bravely, but achieved nothing. The submarine that followed me hit a mine and was lost with all hands. Eventually all our surviving troops surrendered. Churchill refused to acknowledge that the operation was a foredoomed disaster and said it had had great value in convincing the neutral Turks of our offensive spirit. In fact, the down-to-earth Turks were far from impressed by this resound-

---

* Hezlet: Wingfield left Beirut on 9 August and landed two agents before going on to the Dardanelles.

ing defeat, which reinforced their decision not to join what looked like the losing side.

We had one curious encounter which might have turned out badly, but we got away with it. A certain small cargo ship called *Helena* was a regular trader in the Aegean. Several of our submarines had fired torpedoes at her but always missed. One day* I was called to the periscope and there was *Helena* steaming towards us escorted by several small anti-submarine vessels. I immediately set up the attack procedure and ordered two torpedoes to be got ready. Slowly she approached us, much too slowly, and slowly we got nearer and nearer to her line of advance. You cannot stop in a submarine so what I should have done was to speed up, cross her bows, and fire the stern torpedoes. Unfortunately these were not ready and the upshot was that *Helena*'s bow struck our periscope standards and knocked them sideways. Being now blind I broke off the attack and made for the shelter of the nearby Turkish island of Tenedos. The escorts dropped a few ineffective depth charges and once again *Helena* completed her voyage safely. I was the target for some ribald comments when I limped into Beirut, but I had a ready answer: 'You all missed her – at least I hit her, if only with my periscope standards.'

About this time I was delighted to receive the Distinguished Service Cross, the citation referring to 'The sinking of much valuable enemy shipping and the carrying out of four bombardments.' One of these must have been the resin factory which I put out of action with our 4-inch gun. This may not have assisted the war effort much, but the gun's crew enjoyed it and I had no regrets. The resin is used by the Greeks to give a nasty flavour to their wine, which they called retsina. The taste has been acquired over hundreds of years from the coating of the ancient wine jars, or amphoras, with resin to make them winetight. My flotilla commander commented that the submarine gun is not provided for the purpose of relieving the boredom of a dull patrol, and bombardments must be confined to worthwhile targets.

The account which follows is based on an article I wrote some time later.

---

* Hezlet: 22 August.

BULGARS ON HORSEBACK (AUGUST 1943)

On one patrol in 1943 we found ourselves in the North Aegean near the Greek–Bulgarian frontier, not far from the Darda-nelles. We decided to have a look at a small port called Nea Plavia which we en-tered on the surface as it was much too shallow to dive. The harbour was full

Captain Mervyn R.G. Wingfield (left) with Lieutenant John Gibson RNVR

and our trusty gun-layer, Leading Seaman Starbuck, soon sank half a dozen ships. (We always called them 'ships' if they were not actually rowing.) The range was very short and Starbuck could put a row of hits along the waterline without much trouble. The gunnery officer, Lieuten-ant John Gibson RNVR, gave the usual spotting orders – 'Up 200, Right 4, Down 100' etc., but I don't think his contribution was very effective. I'm almost sure I heard Starbuck say, 'Why don't you shut up!'[50]

We had almost completed sending the local merchant navy to permanent diving stations when we were surprised to hear a clatter of hooves. Coming down the mountainside in a cloud of dust was a squadron of cavalry in dress uniforms with pennons flying and lances at the ready. When they reached the quayside the Bulgarian Life Guards, for such they were, unloaded Point 5 machine guns from the animals' backsides and opened fire, much to our consternation. Soon the air was full of flying lead making those 'whipp' noises which mean they have missed you.

At the Charge of the Light Brigade Lord Cardigan found himself alone and surrounded by Russians who attacked him fiercely. In his memoirs he writes, 'It being no part of the duties of a General to cross swords with private soldiers, I turned my horse and left the battlefield.' It occurred to me that it was no part of the duty of a sub-marine to fight with horsed cavalry, so I turned to seaward and rang down Full Speed.

Abaft the bridge on the T-class there was a 20 mm Oerlikon, which had been firing steadily at the Household Cavalry. (This was one of the few occasions when this quick-firing gun did not jam after a few rounds.)

But suddenly our firing ceased. I was surprised to see our Oerlikon gunner coming forward on to the bridge. I asked him what he was doing and he replied, 'I am wounded and I am going to see the coxswain.' I pointed out that he was not wounded very badly and one wasn't supposed to leave one's gun in the middle of a battle. He insisted that he was entitled to have his wound dressed. There was some surprise when he arrived in the control room and I am told that the comments of the crew were critical to say the least of it.

By this time we had sustained a number of half-inch holes in the upperworks. Personally I was all right as I was standing behind the forward periscope. The officer of the watch, Gibson, who was slimmer than me was sheltering behind the after periscope. I told him to take over the Oerlikon. With no more protest than 'Who, *me*, Sir?' he took his seat at the gun. Taking careful aim he fired half a pan in the direction of the cavalry. Soon we were out of their range and when we were in deep enough water we dived.

It was my custom after a successful action to take a day's holiday at 100 feet. This appeared in the log as 'Continued patrol, nothing sighted.' It also gave time for our knees to stop knocking together. The coxswain had his own ritual. 'Complaints about the rum again, Sir. I think you ought to taste it.' A couple of inches of neaters tasted pretty good to me.

But what about our wounded gunner? He certainly had a bullet in his foot, so the first thing to do was to inspect the damage, which we did on the wardroom table. The lad was in some pain and the coxswain had already given him a tot. I suggested that he should have another one, and that the operating team should have one too to steady their nerves at this testing time.

The medical kit supplied to HM submarines contains a number of lancets and scalpels, also a saw similar to the one on view in HMS *Victory* but rather smaller. I hacked away at the foot but the instruments were not sharp and would not cut the flesh satisfactorily. Sterner measures were clearly necessary so I got a Gillette razor blade (a new one of course –

nothing unhygienic about *Taurus*) and made a series of longitudinal cuts down the foot avoiding the metatarsal bones as far as possible. We got the bullet out in the end with a pair of pliers and bound up the wound with an ample dose of M&B 293, now known as penicillin.

The patient was by now making loud protests as the rum had not completely dulled his senses. He was also worried by what his messmates were saying. 'Left your gun in action', 'Cowardice in the face of the enemy' and 'I expect the captain will shoot you in the morning' were some of their remarks.

We put him in his bunk and I had some discussion with the coxswain as to the proper course of action. He was in favour of a court martial, quoting the case of Dunbar-Nasmith in the Dardanelles in 1915, who had in fact condemned a man to death for some dereliction of duty. 'You put the prisoner on the casing in front of the gun-platform and then have four men with rifles, only one of which has a bullet in it, the rest are blank. So nobody knows who fires the fatal shot.'

We decided to defer the decision till the morning. Our poor wounded man had a bad night and was much taunted by the crew with blood-curdling accounts of the fate in store for him. In fact he was in such a state of nerves that we all decided he had had enough. The coxswain told him he was lucky and the captain had decided to spare his life. We eventually got him to a hospital where he made a good recovery, but the doctor said that it was a curious wound. He couldn't understand how the man got all those long cuts down his foot.

There were several similar actions in World War I, but I think this was the only case in World War II where a submarine fought with Bulgars on horseback.*

---

* Hezlet: *Taurus* was on patrol in the approaches to Volos in the Aegean when on 8th July she fired four torpedoes at a small escorted supply ship claiming two hits. The ship stopped and no counter attack developed but before *Taurus* could finish her off, the ship got under way and escaped into harbour. *Taurus* then sank two caiques and next day she fired two torpedoes into a harbour on the island of Lemnos and sank four caiques alongside, before opening bombardment with her gun and setting buildings on fire. *Taurus* then moved to Nea Plavia near Potidea in Euboea, a place where chrome is loaded into caiques, and on 11th fired a torpedo at the pier but it passed through the supports without exploding. Again she bombarded the place and hit a warehouse and sank a tug and no less than ten caiques.

SINKING CAIQUES

Much of our time in the Aegean was spent in sinking caiques (a sailing cargo ship). These picturesque vessels were used for shipping stores to the enemy garrisons on the different islands and were usually under sail. They were legitimate targets but it was disagreeable work.*

We sank one off Mitylene which, according to the chart, was formerly Lesbos.[51] We took three of the crew on board and set course for our base. I made the usual signal for requirements on arrival concluding with 'Request accommodation for three Lesbian survivors'.

We were based on Beirut because of the loss of HMS *Medway*, our luxurious depot ship, which had been sunk on the way from Alexandria (which was being evacuated in anticipation of the fall of Egypt to Rommel's Afrika Korps). The U-boat which sank the *Medway* made an excellent attack, evaded two good escorts and sent her to the bottom with two well-placed torpedoes. Most of the crew were survivors but an enormous quantity of valuable stores were lost, including many spare torpedoes.

Among those picked up was the paymaster commander, who nearly drowned clutching the ship's account books. This must have been why, a year later, I received a handsome cheque from the Medway Wine Fund account which was kept in an English bank. The size of one's share depended on how much one had supported the bar in previous years. This was in marked contrast to the distribution of the Naval Prize Fund in 1945. Our ancestors had become rich from Prize Money but not us. My allocation, despite a good score of sinkings, was about £20 – a few pounds less than the commander-in-chief and a few pounds more than the most junior NAAFI assistant. I had bought a car on my expectations but they were grievously disappointed. Mr Attlee, the Prime Minister, did not approve of the system, which he later abolished for ever.

Mention of Mr Attlee reminds me of something which happened just after the war. A rating wrote to the Prime Minister with some

---

* Hezlet: On 10 June Wingfield off Stampalia in the Aegean sighted a U-boat and fired six torpedoes at 4,000 yards but the enemy saw the torpedo tracks, dived and got away. Instead in the period 3–11 June Wingfield sank seven caiques by gunfire.

grievance. The docket came to me and I pointed out that ratings were allowed to write to their own MPs but not directly to the Prime Minister. The rating's CO was told to take the necessary action against him. The rating's defence, however, was impregnable – he lived in Limehouse and the Prime Minister was his MP.

We had a court martial at Beirut at which I had to prosecute my first lieutenant, John Gibson. He was an RNVR officer, like all my officers towards the end of the war. The young regular sub-lieutenants who were attracted to submarines seemed to me to be of progressively lower quality. I much preferred the young RNVRs, who must have been about the cream of the youth of Britain. Anyway I had to court-martial Gibson because he left a top-secret message in a bar. It was picked up by some busybody army major, who, instead of giving it to one of the *Taurus*'s officers, took it to Army HQ. Gibson was convicted of negligence and sentenced to be reprimanded. But he had the last laugh. Some months later we were informed by the Admiralty that as there was no record of Gibson's promotion to lieutenant at the time of his trial, the court martial was declared null and void. Gibson reminded me that he had asked if he might put up a second stripe when he became first lieutenant as it looked a bit silly to be only a sub-lieutenant. Apparently I had agreed.

Sightseeing was good in this part of the Middle East. I had a weekend in Palestine and saw all the sights including Bethlehem, where the legendary American tourist enquired where the steel works were. This was like the American lady at the Acropolis who politely asked me to point out the seven hills on which the city was built. I replied that it was actually Rome that had seven hills. 'So sorry,' she said, 'I got mixed up. Rome was Thursday.'

One interesting visitor to Beirut was Noel Coward. He was on a tour of military posts overseas, entertaining the troops with a one-man show. I had met him before when he stayed a couple of weeks in HMS *Medway* at Hong Kong. He had an affection for the Navy and insisted that the only way to travel was by 'Grey Funnel Line'. As a born actor he played the part of a naval officer perfectly, the grey flannel trousers and soft hat, and preference for pink gin, making him very much one of us. (I believe he disliked pink gin, but made the sacrifice for art's sake.) One day at the Cercle Militaire swimming pool we were astonished to see Noel climbing up to the highest diving board. Could it be he was going to dive from that enormous height? No, he held his nose with one hand and protected himself against shock with the other, and jumped feet first. When he came up he swam over to our table and I asked him what he would like to drink. 'Ouzo, my dear, ouzo please. It's the *only* thing to drink when you are half full of seawater.'

Several staff officers from Cairo used to come to Beirut for a few days' leave. We did our best to show them around and they used to ask us to drop in if we found ourselves in Cairo. Thus it was that when the time came for us to move further east, I decided that a couple of days in Cairo would be fun. I left *Taurus* at Port Said, wishing Gibson a safe voyage to Suez, where I would rejoin the submarine. At Cairo my host was Colonel Philip Astley, formerly CO of the Life Guards and later ADC to the King of Greece. King Paul got away from Greece at the occupation and lived in Cairo under British protection.

Astley was quite a feature of local society, as he had been in London where his wife was a famous actress. Now he carried a blue and white horsehair fly-whisk (the Greek national colours) and knew all the best places and the best people. The Gezira Club, the Mohammed Ali Club where a gloomy King Farouk was sitting at a corner table eyeing the local talent, and of course Shepeard's Hotel, were some of the places we visited. It was hard to believe that a war was being fought not so many miles down the coast.

I rejoined *Taurus* at Suez. All had gone well. The pilot was most competent and they had had no bumps. Thinking about it now I am a little surprised that I left Gibson on his own to take the ship through the canal. I don't think my superiors would have approved but I was getting rather cocky at this time and didn't really care what they thought.

13

TAURUS GOES EAST (1943-44)

TAURUS IN THE INDIAN OCEAN (LATE 1943)

Ceylon, about which the hymn unkindly says 'Though every prospect pleases and only man is vile', was a busy place in 1943. Admiral Mountbatten had his HQ at Kandy, where he was planning the invasion of Malaya. Our submarines were based at first at Colombo and later at Trincomalee, where there was a considerable fleet of warships and supply vessels. There was a rest camp at Diyatalawa which included a golf course, and a resort in the hills called Nuwara Elia where one could enjoy a weekend in a cool climate – they even had log fires in the evenings.

Our depot ship was HMS *Maidstone*, similar to *Medway* but with every modern facility for our comfort and the efficient maintenance of submarines. Jackie Slaughter, a great character, was the captain and flotilla commander. Among many other sterling qualities, he was a formidable liar dice player. (This is a form of poker played with dice.) Many a time we played till the small hours, always with the same result – Jackie finishing up with a large pile of rupees in front of him.[52]

One morning at Colombo I was pacing the quarterdeck of *Maidstone* after breakfast when we saw approaching the harbour entrance a fine-looking trading schooner under full sail, flying the flag of the Maharajah of Travancore. Suddenly there was a muffled explosion and she blew up, masts and rigging flying in every direction. Within a minute there was nothing left but some floating wreckage and a few survivors in the water.

We assumed she had been torpedoed and were somewhat alarmed, but the explanation was quite different – *we* had blown her up. It seems that Colombo was protected by a controlled minefield. If a U-boat passed over the sensitive instruments on the sea bottom a warning was given to the control officer ashore, who could then detonate a mine and blow up the U-boat. On this occasion the officer received a strong signal but saw only a wooden sailing ship. He assumed that a U-boat was *under* the schooner and pressed the button with the results which we saw. In fact, there was no U-boat but the schooner was laden with iron ore, which accounted for the violent swing of the galvanometer. His Highness of Travancore was said to be very cross about the incident. Another morning in Trincomalee, the submarine *Severn* was alongside *Maidstone* and the crew were engaged in firing watershots from the torpedo tubes. This was done periodically to test the firing system, there being of course no torpedo in the tube. But on this occasion someone had blundered. There *was* a torpedo in the tube. At 40 knots it sped across the crowded harbour and struck an Admiralty oil tanker amidships, blowing a large hole in her side. Tankers don't sink easily due to their many compartments so no great harm was done except perhaps to the reputation of the *Severn*'s torpedo officer.

Trinco harbour was ideal for water picnics. One could borrow one of *Maidstone*'s picket boats and invite a few of the nurses from the naval hospital for an afternoon's aquaplaning. One nurse was not very expert and seemed unable to stand up on the board. Terrified, she knelt on it clutching the sides. As the boat went faster and faster the spray slowly washed off her shoulder straps and gradually her bathing dress slipped lower and lower. Of course we slowed down at once – or nearly at once.

Between patrols we were often guests of tea planters, who lived very comfortable but rather lonely lives only relieved by the Saturday evening drive of perhaps 40 miles to the nearest club. One estate was on the upper slopes of Adams Peak. One Sunday morning we sat on the terrace looking out on a spectacular view of half of Ceylon and drinking, of all things, vintage port. Normally you only drink port after you have had all sorts of other drinks but as the first drink of the day it tastes delicious.

I started off badly in the Malayan area by missing an important ship. I had failed to sink an easy target in the Aegean owing to the torpedoes running under the ship and not exploding. We were forced to use a magnetic pistol on the warhead at the time. The CCR, as it was called, was developed in Britain and worked well in trials. But the trials were in a cold Scottish loch and in the warmer waters of the Mediterranean and the Indian Ocean they failed as often as not. Like most of my colleagues I refused to use them after being let down once, much to the annoyance of the scientists who insisted the CCR was perfect and that we were just bad shots.

My second failure was my own responsibility but resulted from a mistake by a sub-lieutenant. We had news of a troopship which would arrive at Nicobar at dawn. (We had for some time been privy to the Japanese codes, but our knowledge had to be kept secret. Equally we had broken the German ciphers and thus Churchill knew of the impending raid on Coventry. He decided not to warn the inhabitants of that city for fear of compromising our possession of the key.)

Sure enough the troopship appeared at the predicted time and I took my first periscope range of her at 17,000 yards. This being beyond the scale of the plotting chart, which only catered for ranges up to 10,000 yards, my navigator halved the scale to accommodate the longer range. I took ranges every three minutes and they all added up to the same speed – 16 knots. I queried this and the sub invited me to check the plot without disclosing that he had halved the scale. Sure enough I made it 16 knots. With some misgivings and contrary to my observations of the bow wave which indicated a much lower speed, I fired four torpedoes spread over three lengths of the ship. All missed far ahead as the ship was only doing 8 knots. Her two escorting destroyers creamed down the tracks all too visible in the glassy sea and gave us a well-deserved pasting. I think it was during the depth-charging that a rating passed a form to the coxswain on which was written 'Request to see the Captain to be transferred to general service.' It wasn't actually all that bad and after a few hours they gave up and we surfaced at dusk to an empty sea, almost undamaged. My only plea in mitigation for failing to spot the mistake is that I was suffering from flu and had a temperature of 102°.*

I put the sub-lieutenant under arrest and relieved him of all duties. I had to relax this a few days later when the other two officers complained of being 'watch and watch' – i.e. four hours on and four hours off. The young sub, whose brother had been a most successful submarine CO in the early days of the war, was put ashore on return from this patrol but was given another chance in another submarine. His new CO sacked him as incompetent after just one patrol and he was reverted to general service to pass the rest of the war in a battleship.

After the run of failures I was almost relieved of my command, and would have been but for the intervention of the second-in-command of the flotilla, Commander 'Ginger' Cavenagh-Mainwaring.[53] He had been a successful CO in the early days and pleaded for me to be given another chance. Perhaps I did not help myself by remarking late at night in the wardroom that I was damned if I was going to accept criticism of the conduct of my patrol from a captain who had never heard a shot fired or a depth-charge exploded in either war. One of the group I was with was his secretary, who probably related my words to his master next morning. Thus it was that I was slightly under a cloud when we sailed on our next patrol. But I am pleased to say this turned out to be my finest hour.

TAURUS IN THE FAR EAST (NOVEMBER 1943 – MAY 1944)

We had warning of a Japanese U-boat which was due to enter Penang harbour around sunrise. On 13 November I positioned myself near the end of the searched channel, just off the port. Our target, the *I.34*, was a large submarine and appeared in the darkness just before dawn and only just visible in the early light. I started the attack on the

---

*   Hezlet: On her next patrol *Taurus* left Trincomalee on 15th December to land agents in the Nicobar Islands, where she patrolled until 23rd when she was ordered to Pulo Weh. On Christmas Day she sighted an escorted merchant ship. She closed and fired six torpedoes at a range of 3500 yards but all missed ahead.

surface but increasing light forced me to dive. The light was not strong enough to see anything through the periscope so I had to depend on Asdic or sonar for my bearings of the target. With little hope of success I fired six torpedoes spread over five lengths, reckoning that one hit was enough to sink a U-boat. We heard explosions but were uncertain of the result. I reported a possible sinking. In fact, I had sunk her with one torpedo right under the periscope standards. She sank instantly and we crept away from the scene to spend a quiet day, enlivened by a big tot of rum from the coxswain, who was convinced we had hit her.*

At dusk we surfaced, to find that there was a Japanese anti-submarine chaser rather close. All night we went at our best speed while charging the batteries and our shadow followed us at a discreet distance. Dawn came and we had to dive. We were in rather too shallow water and we stuck on the bottom, bows in the mud at about 150 feet. Our enemy repeatedly passed over us, dropping depth charges. I knew which class of ship she was and after twenty-four depth charges I told the crew that that was all they had. I was answered by a thunderous salvo of another six, which did us some damage. Feeling that there was no future in sitting on the bottom being slowly destroyed, I ordered 'Gun action!' and blew all the tanks. We surfaced and there was our attacker about 1,000 yards away on a parallel course.

My superb gun's crew opened fire within about 21 seconds of surfacing and quickly knocked out the enemy's only gun. Leading Seaman Starbuck then put a number of shells along her waterline which put her out of action. At that time I did something I had never done before. I hit a rating in the small of the back as hard as I could. He was supposed to be an anti-aircraft lookout but he was watching the gunnery as if it were a football match. 'Good shot, guns!' he shouted, 'Put another one in the stern.'

---

* Wingfield has placed these events out of sequence, according to Hezlet: *Taurus* arrived from the Mediterranean on 12 October with her periscopes damaged during her last patrol in the Aegean. They were replaced in time to leave for patrol on 6 November. She was ordered to patrol off Penang where before dawn on 13th she sighted a large U-boat in between rainsqualls and fired six torpedoes at a range of 5000 yards, sinking the Japanese.

Up-sun was a Japanese aircraft just flipping its wings to make a dive on us. I pressed the diving hooter while the gun was still firing and the crew all scrambled below in good time. I was a little late in getting down and arrived in the control room with half a ton of seawater. My charming first lieutenant said, 'Sir, please don't do that again. It's so bad for the electrics.'

Some while later the *Illustrated London News* carried a two-page spread featuring this action. Many years later, in the 1970s, the *I.34* was salvaged from the sea bed and found to contain 9 tons of gold and 12 tons of tin which had been destined for support of the German war effort. The Japanese captain's ceremonial sword was also found and this was kindly presented to me. I passed it on the Submarine Museum in Gosport.[54]

Their Lordships of the Admiralty were rather pleased about this smart little battle and gave me a bar to my DSC. I recommended the usual number of members of the crew for DSMs, choosing the heads of departments, since there was no way in which a member of a submarine crew could show gallantry. They either did their job satisfactorily or I sacked them. One man, Chief Stoker Ralfs, was put in for a gong for the second time. I had recommended him some months before but nothing happened, so I put him in again. Much to his surprise a few weeks later he received the DSM and bar by the same post.[55]

Ralfs had another distinction, rare for a chief stoker – he received a head wound from a splinter during a gun battle. Don't ask me why the chief stoker was on the bridge during the action – I expect he was just an interested spectator. Anyway, it fell to me to deal with his wound – a three-inch cut down his forehead. I sewed him up the best I could, but I admit it was a bit rough. However, the wound healed well although the scar was rather noticeable. Twenty years later I was in the Links Hotel, Liphook, when a large Jaguar drew up and a prosperous-looking man entered the bar. I did not at first notice the scar down his forehead but when he greeted me the penny dropped. It was, of course, Ralfs. I asked him what job he had. 'I've been lucky,' he answered. 'I am now area manager for British Leyland Motors.' It is a great pleasure when old friends reach the top of their tree.

The department called Honours and Awards made some extraordinary decisions during the war. Reputedly it was headed by a cavalry colonel's widow called Mrs Golightly, who was a little out of touch. It must be realised that senior officers merely send a citation and a recommendation for an award (except in the case of the VC which has special rules), and leave it to the Honours and Awards to allot the particular award, which may be a DSO, DSC or a Mention in Despatches. All of us preferred to have a DSO and a DSC rather than two DSOs because you can't go round telling everyone that you have a bar. At least two submariners received three DSOs, i.e. DSO and two bars and nothing else. Commander 'Baldy' Hezlet already had the DSO twice and the DSC three times when he had a tremendous success in the Java Sea. He sank a Japanese cruiser in a brilliant action which the Americans marked by the award of their highest decoration available to foreigners, the Legion of Merit, Degree of Officer. Our commander-in-chief recommended the immediate award of the VC, but Mrs Golightly thought otherwise. It takes about six weeks to get a VC approved. Mrs Golightly considered it was essential to match the American medal with no delay so the result was that Hezlet received yet another DSO. He would not have minded waiting a bit for a VC.

There were some other odd stories about medals. One friend of mine torpedoed a U-boat in the southern North Sea in the early days of the war. His claim was disallowed by the Admiralty but post-war analysis showed that he *had* sunk the U-boat at the exact time and place he had reported. He was awarded a DSC, which was rather mean, since in 1939 the reward for sinking a U-boat was a DSO. However, he had made up for it in the meantime with a couple of other gongs.

Perhaps the luckiest chap to win a DSO was a destroyer captain who got appendicitis just before the Dunkirk evacuation. His first lieutenant assumed command and did a first-class job evacuating the army. In due course his ex-CO, still languishing in Haslar Hospital, received a DSO. He protested and offered to return it at once but this was not accepted. You cannot withdraw a medal once awarded, they said. However, they decided to give the first lieutenant one too. Mrs Golightly must have been in a benevolent mood.

I was delighted to get a DSC for my engineer officer for a fine piece of work. As mentioned earlier, after sinking the Japanese U-boat *I.34* we suffered quite a bit of damage from a prolonged depth-charging. In fact we had no steering, which was awkward when we had to surface. However, this young officer, an RNVR as it happened, crept aft into the extreme stern and closed a bypass valve which had opened due to shock, and thus restored power to the hydraulic steering system. We all thought we were going to be sunk quite soon so it took a lot of courage to go right into the after end. It also showed a good professional knowledge in diagnosing exactly what was wrong.

The one medal we all despised was the so-called 1939–45 Star. Originally this was the 1939 Star but somebody in the government, probably Attlee, thought this discriminated in favour of regulars and volunteers. The change in its scope meant that everybody, even the last conscript called up in 1945, received it, which made it worthless. I refused to wear it for some years until sharply spoken to by an admiral.

Our crew in *Taurus* naturally collected a lot of medals. I was taught the art of writing citations by a World War I veteran who criticised my style. I had written, 'This rating performed his duties well in this action and is worthy of commendation.' My friend tore this up and wrote, 'This rating's conduct in battle was an inspiration to the whole crew. His cheerfulness and devotion to duty in exceptionally arduous circumstances contributed in large measure to the successful conclusion of the operation.'

'Try that,' he said, 'I bet he gets something.'

The first DSM awarded to a member of *Taurus*'s crew I gave to Petty Officer Steward Knowles, my personal steward. He was a splendid character, always ready with a hot meal or an iced drink and a stalwart member of the ammunitions supply team, his job being to pass shells up from the magazine to the gun's crew.[56] Those iced drinks were important. When you are very frightened, as I was all too frequently, three things happen. You suddenly feel very thirsty, you have a desire to pee every few minutes and your knees start knocking together. The solution is to cross your legs and have a drink of iced water.

The story I like best is of the army colonel who concluded his battle report '… and finally I would like to recommend my batman, Private Atkins, for the VC. During a long engagement, in the face of fierce fire from the enemy, Atkins showed exemplary courage and devotion to duty, following me everywhere I went.'

My time in submarines was the most important of my life and left deep impressions. Many people have said to me, 'Oh, I couldn't bear to go to sea in a submarine, I should get claustrophobia.' I never met a submariner who suffered from this trouble. If there were any, they must have been diverted from submarines at an early stage. It's mainly a matter of training. Steeplejacks and men working on skyscrapers are not particularly brave. They don't suffer from vertigo because they are trained to act normally at great heights. If you go into submarines at the age of twenty you soon get used to the cramped surroundings.

Fear is something I became well acquainted with during the war years. I believe most people feel fear to about the same extent. But the trained man doesn't show it and doesn't let it influence his actions. Surprisingly, it doesn't seem to matter much what he is trained for. The weapons may be wrong, the tactics may be wrong, but if a man is trained for the military business, he is ten times as good as an untrained man. To use an army analogy, foot-drill (or square bashing) has no practical value but a regiment which is good on parade is usually better in action than one which has a sloppy attitude. The Life Guards are trained on horses but nobody criticises their performance in tanks.

For the next few months I had a run of small successes. One was a freighter with a cargo of timber. Gunfire and even a torpedo had little effect except to start a fire which caused the crew to jump overboard. I tried to pick them up but in the best Japanese tradition they preferred death, which they achieved by diving into our revolving propellers. One man, however, climbed onto our stern and I reported triumphantly that I had a Japanese survivor on board. This was a valuable prize and rarely come by. We hurried back to Ceylon, keeping our prisoner alive by every drug we could think of (he was quite badly wounded). A fast launch met us 100 miles out and he was hurried off to the interrogation centre. It was disappointing to hear that he turned out to be a Korean and was thus of no use for intelligence purposes.

Another time we sank a ferry boat off Port Blair, in the Andaman Islands, which I was not particularly proud of, although it did have an armed escort. I was carrying a couple of army commandos at that time and I sent them on board to take the Japanese ensign, which I thought would make a nice trophy. In spite of our shouted directions they failed to locate it as it was hidden by the awning. An aircraft then appeared and we had to recall the men quickly and dive without the souvenir.

We did, however, do an interesting operation in the area involving a detachment of Gurkhas and Indian Army soldiers. We landed them – about thirty men and three officers – on the west coast of the main Andaman island, where they were to conduct a reconnaissance in preparation for the forthcoming invasion of Malaya. The officers entertained us on the voyage with accounts of life as Indian Cavalry officers in pre-war days. It sounded most enjoyable – little work, masses of servants, big game hunting with, of course, polo as the ruling passion.

Landing them was quite funny as they were a most un-nautical lot. One Gurkha fell into the sea while boarding the rubber dinghy. With his rifle and heavy pack he was immediately in difficulties. Lieutenant Gibson jumped in and rescued him from drowning while his comrades roared with laughter. Most men would have dropped their rifle in these circumstances but he clung on to his and would have gone down with it. Fine soldiers, these little men.*

We used to let a few of them onto the bridge at night for a breath of fresh air. One of them made a remark to his officer in Gurkhali. I asked what he had said. 'Oh, he just asked which way we were going,' replied the officer.

This party had a fine assortment of weapons including rifles with silencers and steel crossbows. The latter were very popular and accounted for quite a few Japanese sentries. 'Lethal at 50 yards, silent

---

*   Hezlet: *Taurus* and *Trespasser* left Trincomalee for patrol in January, and landed 12 men and 9000 lbs of stores in the Andamans on 23rd, then on 6th February, *Taurus* shifted to the south west coast of Sumatra and sank a tug and a lighter by gunfire.

and economical. When you have killed the man you can pull out the arrow and use it again,' I was told. They took quite a load of provisions with them which they buried for safety. But the wild natives, called Juwarus, must have been watching them for the whole lot was stolen the first night. Thereafter they lived by their guns and fishing rods and suffered little discomfort, or so they said. However, they terrorised the Japanese garrison, who gave up any activity outside their fortified camps.

A profitable use of submarines, which might well have been used much more, was mine-laying. We had several special mine-laying submarines which could lay a field of fifty or more mines, but they were too large and cumbersome and were little used in their specialist roles. One of them, HM Submarine *Seal*, was even captured intact by the Germans, but they never took her to sea. They called her the 'iron coffin'. It was possible, however, to discharge specially designed mines from torpedo tubes. It was *where* you laid your mines, not how many, that counted and a submarine could lay a few mines at some focal point such as off a headland or in the approach channel of a port with an excellent chance of catching a ship or two. Of course the depth of water had to be right as they were magnetic mines.*

I laid six mines just off the One Fathom Bank Buoy in the Malacca Strait where the channel is both narrow and shallow, and another group at the entrance to the Penang searched channel. I was told later that they accounted for several ships but details were lacking and the tonnage was not credited to my score as surely it should have been.**
Nor were any gongs awarded for mine-laying, however successful. Perhaps this accounted for the unpopularity of this form of warfare with most submariners, though not with me. I received a Mention in Despatches about this time but with no clues as to what it was for![57]

---

*   Hezlet: *Taurus* was armed with the M Mark II mine, a 1000-lb ground magnetic mine laid from the torpedo tubes.

**   Hezlet: On his last patrol in the Far East Wingfield sailed on 12th April with twelve M Mark II mines (in place of two torpedoes) embarked, which he laid off Penang on 18th. He saw a U-boat approaching but too late to obtain a firing solution. On 22nd April he engaged a tug towing a salvage vessel and fired two torpedos by eye but missed. His mines sank the *Kasumi Maru* of 1400 tons on 12th May.

TAURUS HOMEWARD BOUND (MAY – JULY 1944)

Targets were getting scarce in 1944. I did a couple more patrols and sank some small stuff on the west coast of Sumatra. I even surprised the inhabitants of Belem (now called something else), at the southern tip near the Sunda Strait, with a visit, but to no good purpose. We returned to Trinco flying a string of flags like a Cowes Week winner and prepared to sail for England. I told the crew that we were going home, which was a most welcome piece of news to all but one of my audience. 'Home,' he said. 'Don't talk to me about home. I was brought up in one.'

We called at Aden on the way back, where I was invited by the admiral to join him in an interesting operation. This was the same admiral who had sent his flag lieutenant to the dockside to welcome an armed trawler which had captured an Italian submarine intact earlier in the war. 'The Admiral would like you to come to dinner tonight. I have a car here and will run you up,' said Flags. 'I'm sorry, young man,' said the north country skipper. 'I can't coom to dinner. Ah've joost 'ad big tea.'

Our operation concerned the German U-boat *U-852* commanded by Kapitänleutnant Eck. This was one of the few U-boats deployed in the Indian Ocean and Eck was told to keep his presence secret as far as possible. He sank the Greek ship *Peleus* off the coast of Africa and machine-gunned the survivors in the lifeboats. But not all were killed. Three survived and told their story, including the number of the U-boat, to the authorities at Aden. The *U-852* was hunted strenuously and was eventually damaged by an RAF Hudson to such an extent that it could no longer dive. Eck tried to escape by running his ship ashore on the coast of Italian Somaliland, but it was not, as he thought, a friendly country. The British had conquered it some time before. Eck and his crew were quickly rounded up by the Camel Corps – an unlikely fate for a U-boat crew.[58]

The admiral and I flew to the wreck which we found intact but thoroughly looted – not a single pair of binoculars in sight. Before taking to the desert, Eck had collected all his secret documents and signal code, put them in a weighted bag and dropped them over the side. Thus we found all we wanted in one neat package on the seabed alongside the ship.[59]

Eck was court-martialled in 1945 and pleaded 'superior orders' as his defence. He asked several well-known U-boat commanders to speak for him but they all refused. They considered he had transgressed the code of honour of the U-boat Corps. He was executed by firing squad – the only U-boat commander to be charged with a war crime. Cases of shooting survivors had occurred in our Navy and an appalling case in the Pacific involving a US Navy submarine attracted some attention but no action was taken against the COs concerned. In Eck's case the moral (if that is the right word) seems to be that if you are going to shoot survivors, make sure you kill all of them.

Malta was our next stop, where we were warmly welcomed. The hectic days of the siege were long past and life was fairly normal. We berthed alongside HM Submarine *Trenchant*, commanded by my friend Baldy Hezlet, who was on his way out to the Pacific. When the time came for us to sail for Britain there was quite a crowd on the jetty to wave us goodbye. I shook hands with everybody, went up to the bridge and gave the order to let go.

'Sir,' said the coxswain. 'Someone has taken the steering wheel.' An embarrassing pause ensued with the spectators longing to get back to their breakfasts, while I directed search parties in all directions. Eventually it was found being used as the centrepiece of *Trenchant*'s wardroom table. To this day Baldy Hezlet insists he has no idea how it got there.

On the next leg of the voyage we were put in the middle of a convoy bound for Britain. We had an immense Sunderland flying boat as escort which circled the convoy ceaselessly. When its patrol was completed it flew low down the starboard column of the convoy waving its wings as a goodbye gesture. We were horrified to see the anti-aircraft gunners on the last ship of the column open fire and shoot down this fine aircraft. There was often bad blood between the RAF and the RN but it was not all the fault of the RAF.

Eventually we reached England and with something of a sigh of relief turned the boat over to the dockyard, somewhat battered but intact.

14

PEACE (1945)

AROUND THE WORLD AND BACK AGAIN

The year 1945 saw me established on the staff of Flag Officer Submarines at his headquarters in a block of flats at Swiss Cottage. We had a good view of the occasional rocket, V-1 or V-2, falling on London. My admiral, Sir George Creasy, was a colourful character who made use of a wealth of metaphors which often kept his listeners, particularly Americans, quite in the dark as to what he meant. Once I was in the Holy of Holies, the Board Room of the Admiralty, sitting behind my boss with a file of supporting documents. 'Gentlemen,' said Sir George, 'if we bury our heads in the sand we shall be riding for a fall.' I caught the eye of a friendly civil servant the other side of the table and we both made a note of this one for our collections. We were often enjoined to keep our shoulders to the wheel and our ears to the ground, although progress must be difficult in this posture.[60]

When he went on a world tour he took his chief of staff, Captain G. C. Phillips, formerly of the Harwich flotilla, and me as flag lieutenant. We went right round the world eastwards, flying all the way except from San Francisco to New York, which we did the leisurely way, by train, the admiral saying he was tired of flying. We went across India in the Viceroy's private plane, stopping for a night at Delhi and at Madras. At the latter, it was pleasant to meet my brother-in-law, Captain Hugh Mundy, who was commanding the RN Air Station.[61]

A long hop in a Catalina flying boat (the Kangaroo Service) from Colombo took us to Perth, West Australia. We were somewhat overloaded but I took comfort from the fact that we had two engines and could land on the sea. 'Much good that will do you,' said the pilot. 'On one engine we can't reach Australia and all the islands in between are Japanese occupied.'

My visit to Australia was compressed into ten days and included brief visits to Perth, Fremantle, Melbourne, Sydney and Brisbane. We did not see very much of the real Australia nor meet a true cross-section of the people, but what I saw I liked very much. The light-hearted and irreverent attitude of young Australians makes them stimulating companions. We stayed aboard the ubiquitous HMS *Maidstone* at Perth, then at the Melbourne Club and the Royal Sydney Yacht Squadron.

In the Pacific we were guests of the US Navy, who treated us well, even placing a bottle of bourbon in the Admiral's cabin, contrary to all their regulations. By mischance all our bags were sent to the wrong island so that when we boarded Admiral Lockwood's flagship at Guam we had no suitable clothes. This was soon remedied when we were equipped from the US Navy stores with smart and practical suits of khaki and every other requirement, down to toothbrushes. When Admiral Lockwood published his book on the submarine war in the Pacific he mentioned me personally. My little niche in American naval history reads as follows: 'The Flag Lieutenant, MR Wingfield, made the mistake of sending all the baggage of the party by Military Air Transport to Midway Island instead of Guam, which caused some inconvenience to Admiral Creasy when he arrived on board my flagship.' This, of course, was grossly unfair to me. All the blame rested with the Military Air Transport dispatchers, although I doubt if they would admit it.[62]

At one party, probably in Hawaii, I found myself in conversation with a US Air Force Colonel. I seem to remember laying down the law about how bombing alone could never win a war. My companion looked thoughtful and said, 'It could, you know. It just could.' His name was Colonel Le May and a few months later he dropped the atom bomb on Hiroshima. In due course he became head of the USAF and I had the pleasure of renewing his acquaintance in Washington. He remembered our conversation. 'You sure got that one wrong, Commander,' he said with some satisfaction.

Anyone who reads the Sunday supplements knows all about the South Pacific. We had our share of waving palm trees, beach picnics, rum cocktails and even surfing at Waikiki beach. When we left Hawaii there was quite a large party to see us off. We shook hands with everybody, floral garlands were placed around our necks and off we flew. Two hours later, we were back again with engine trouble. Our hosts welcomed us again and took us off to a party. Hard as it may be to believe, the same thing happened the next day. Few people saw us off on our fourth departure, this time in a Pan American Clipper, the most civilised aircraft I have ever travelled in. I remarked to the bar steward, who was English, that it was nice to know that we could land on the ocean. 'I suppose it is a theoretical advantage, but in our seventeen years of operating this service, Pan American has never had a forced landing,' he told me somewhat coldly.

Much refreshed after three days in a luxury train, we arrived in New York. Among those who looked after us was a well-known American yachtsman called Paul Hammond, who had a romantic feeling about the Royal Navy, in which I believe he had served in World War I. He sent us off to the Rockefeller Center, where the famous Rockettes showed us what chorus dancing can be, and then to dinner at the 21 Club. At first we had a cold reception and were placed at a miserable table near the pantry hatch, but when his phone call arrived to say the bill was on him we were instantly moved to an excellent table. The place was pretty empty but we could see Greta Garbo, all alone, at the next table but one. Next to us was a plump dowager who, when asked what she wished to order, said, 'I'll have exactly what Miss Garbo is having.'[63]

Back in England VE Day arrived. By this time I had become a member of the United Service Club, known as the Senior. Alas, it is no more. If you should visit the Institute of Directors, look around you. This was the club founded in 1815 for senior officers of both services. At first the Duke of Wellington opposed it, saying that if all those generals and admirals got together they would surely plot revolution.

But evidently he softened his attitude because there is a mounting-block outside the old front door on which is the inscription, 'Erected by the desire of the Duke of Wellington'.

I tried to keep the bar open a little later than usual on VE night. I and an American friend had been outside Buckingham Palace and felt that victory needed celebrating. 'Closing time, gentlemen,' called Mr Hughes, the chief steward. 'But we have just won a war. Surely we can have one for the road?' But he was adamant. War or peace, rules were rules and not to be broken for any frivolous reason.

In 1945 I met the famous Edwardian character Rosa Lewis, whose career was so well fictionalised by the BBC in the series *The Duchess of Duke Street*. Rosa was of fairly humble origin but was distinguished by considerable beauty and great talent as a cook. She made a name for herself as a sort of jobbing cook who would come to the house of some famous hostess and prepare the gargantuan feast which was the fashion among that generation of gourmands. Not least of these was Edward, Prince of Wales, later King Edward VII. Rosa was his mistress briefly, but it was her talents below stairs rather than between the sheets which formed the lasting bond between them. The Prince may have helped to set her up in the Cavendish Hotel, where she reigned over the more raffish element of London society for over fifty years.

Her husband, a shadowy figure, had disappeared some years earlier and when I knew her, the only male member of the staff was an elderly hall porter called Fred, who, with his scruffy little dog, inhabited a converted sedan chair at the entrance to the Cavendish and exercised some control over those who sought its hospitality.

I stayed there for the night several times when duty kept me in London. I much enjoyed the cuisine, which was considerably better than the law allowed in those days of strict rationing. It was said that she received quantities of unrationed game from the Scottish estates of her rich friends. The bedrooms would be considered museum pieces nowadays with their great ewers of water on marble washstands, the copper cans of hot water at the touch of a bell, enormous mahogany bedsteads and every other sign of Victorian opulence. Once I had a room with a grand piano in it which I remarked on jokingly when I paid my bill. Rosa overheard me and in her penetrating voice, which retained more than a trace of cockney, exclaimed 'What's 'e complainin' about then? There's lots of them can play the pianner!'

While Rosa drew the line at Jermyn Street tarts, if the girls her guests brought in were upper-class types, she was not one to worry about marriage lines. She was an arch-snob and the rich or titled could do little wrong. Most evenings she held court in the upper drawing room where she sat on a sort of throne and chatted to her guests, who were all male and all in uniform when I was there. Everyone drank champagne and as the evening wore on I am sure that I was not the only one to wonder who was going to pay the bill. But all was well. Rosa called across to a good-looking, slightly dark-skinned, Grenadier officer, 'You're rich, Mr Jaipur. How about paying for the bubbly?' 'Rosa, I would be delighted to do just that,' replied the Maharajah.

Rosa once asked me about her house in Cowes which had presumably been the gift of some admirer. 'When you see Dickie, ask him if I should sell it. It should fetch a good price right next to the Squadron.' I passed her message on to Admiral Mountbatten shortly afterwards. He said she should sell, which she did, and the house is now the club house of the Royal Corinthian Yacht Club.

In Rosa's young days the house in Cowes was the scene of great high jinks, with expensive games of poker and baccarat available to her friends, many of them members of the Squadron. The wives of the members disapproved of Rosa and would cut her dead in the High Street, but as she said, when they felt the need the countesses were all smiles and were happy to use those facilities at her house which did not exist at the Castle.

One night around the turn of the century, Rosa was entertaining a particularly rowdy party of yachtsmen, when the cry went up: 'Let's bomb the Castle!' With a rush, one and all grabbed the nearest missile including all the chamber pots from Rosa's bedrooms and hurled them over the wall on to the sacred turf of the Squadron lawn. Not surprisingly relations with the Castle were cool. There is, however, a picture of Rosa in the drawing room which even some members are not aware of. In 1895 a very handsome painting was made of all the members grouped outside the Castle. In the foreground is one of the barges from the Royal Yacht *Victoria and Albert* from which are disembarking half a dozen assorted royalty, including the Kaiser and the Tsar of Russia. Almost hidden in the background, standing coyly among a group of members, is the unmistakable figure of Rosa who had evidently been smuggled in by friends. I have been told that efforts were made to have her painted out but there she remains, a happy reminder of a remarkable life.

The last time I saw Rosa was when she must have been in her late eighties. She was sitting quite alone in the entrance to the Berkeley Hotel Buttery. On the table beside her was, inevitably, a bottle of Bollinger.[64]

SURRENDER OF U-BOATS

When Germany surrendered there were over 150 U-boats in commission despite the appalling losses sustained – 784 out of a total of 1,171 having been sunk. Few forces in history can have taken such a beating and still retained their fighting spirit. I was sent to Oslo, Norway, soon after VE Day with the title of Senior Officer (Submarines) Norway, to organise the surrender of the 90-odd U-boats in Norwegian

Surrendered Type 21 U-boat U2502 (flagship on the voyage from Oslo) and a smaller coastal U-boat alongside depot ship at Rothesay, Scotland 1945

ports. I crossed the North Sea in good style, accompanying Crown Prince Olaf, who was to represent his father King Haakon at the victory celebrations. These took the usual form of parades and marches but there were a few unusual features. There were quite a few girls in the ranks and many of the rifles had wild flowers stuck in the barrel. There was even an orange impaled on one soldier's bayonet.

We duly took over the U-boats at Oslo and other officers in my party did the same at Bergen and other ports where there were small flotillas. At first we armed our sailors with carbines but the senior German officer, Korvettenkapitän Schnee, told me it was quite unnecessary. 'My men are disciplined. We have been told to surrender by Berlin and we will carry out our orders. This will be a well-organised operation and we would not like it to be marred by any shooting. Your men appear unfamiliar with their weapons and might easily cause an accident.'[65]

Schnee was an impressive figure with whom I became quite friendly. He had several Iron Crosses as well as the Ritter Cross with diamonds, which he had won for sinking a large tonnage of Allied shipping. 'Many other U-boat commanders received high decorations in the early part of the war when any fool could knock up a good score, but I won all my medals in 1941 and 1942 when things were pretty difficult for us,' he told me with an engaging lack of modesty.

He said we were making a mistake in taking over the U-boats which would be useful to us when we had to fight the Russians, which we certainly would within six months. He insisted that despite their losses, the morale of the U-boat men was high and they were furious at having to surrender just when their new super U-boat, the Type XXI, was ready for service.

I took over one of these as my flagship and I soon realised how lucky we were not to have had to contend with the Type XXI. They were much faster, more heavily armed and could dive twice as deep as the old Type VII C which they were to replace. If the Germans had concentrated on U-boats instead of wasting effort on battleships and vast fleets of bombers, the war would have finished in 1942. I believe they only had forty operational boats in September 1939. If they had had 200, Britain would have been starved into defeat.

Schnee told me that the Type XXI which I had picked up was a bad choice. The captain had been a teetotaller and allowed no liquor on board, unlike the other boats which were well stocked with French wine and Dutch gin. There were enormous stocks of champagne in the German equivalent of the NAAFI in Oslo, all stamped Réservé à la Wehrmacht. We used to send a car every day to the storehouse for a few cases which were *free*. At least they were free until the army commander, General Browning, found out about it and issued an order which is probably unique in army history:

'The free issue of champagne is to cease forthwith. In future a charge of one shilling and sixpence for each bottle is to be made, which will be given to army charities.' In fact, we quickly got tired of the stuff and when a Polish destroyer arrived with a good stock of beer we were happy to do a swap, bottle for bottle.

We were well supplied with staff cars requisitioned from the Germans. Mine was a very nice Mercedes open tourer with which I explored some of Southern Norway. One evening in the hotel an RNVR officer asked me if I would like him to take it to the UK in his landing ship. 'All you have to do is park it on the dockside near my ship and then report it to the Military Police as stolen. I will leave it in some convenient car park when we reach UK and you can collect it. Worth £50, don't you think?' He said he had done it several times and the system worked perfectly. Sorely tempted as I was, bearing in mind the shortage of cars in England, I foresaw difficulties in registration and licensing, and politely declined the offer. Now I don't suppose I shall ever own a Mercedes. Too bad!

Except for a few German technicians who were retained to assist our own men in sailing the boats back to the UK, all the U-boat crews were sent off to a POW camp to await repatriation. I went to the station where a special train was being loaded with the crews. Schnee was there, every inch the Prussian officer, wearing a long grey greatcoat and sporting a monocle. He was a little annoyed with the Norwegian authorities, who apparently expected the officers to go in cattle trucks with the men. I am pleased to say I was able to put this right and proper carriages were provided. Schnee thanked me and said goodbye. 'Here is the address of my schloss in Silesia. I hope you will come and stay with me when all this trouble is sorted out,' he said, adding, 'You had better have my pistol. I shan't be needing it where we are going.' The train drew out. It was a very well-conducted surrender.

Next day I took my handsome new Type XXI to sea for a short trial, to find that they were brutes to handle. To be technical for a moment, I must explain that the propeller shafts pointed outwards 10° from the fore and aft line and the propellers were in-turning. Thus when going alongside starboard, in order to swing in the stern, one had to go astern with the starboard screw – exactly the opposite to every other ship in the world.

I got the hang of it in the end and proudly sailed from Oslo at the head of my flotilla of some twenty-five U-boats. We had no mechanical trouble thanks to our Germans, all of whom were keen to join the Royal Navy! In the wardroom we had the squadron engineer officer who had been in U-boats all the war until recently, when he had been on duty at the construction yard in Hamburg. I asked him about air raids by the RAF. He said they caused no trouble. Few bombs fell anywhere near the U-boats under construction and, anyway, what better air raid shelter could you have than the hull of a U-boat on the stocks?

We joined up with the other U-boats from Bergen and Kristiansand and made an impressive entry into Scapa Flow. Immediately a horde of would-be looters descended on us from the Home Fleet ships. But they were too late. I had told our people that every rating could have one thing and every officer two things. I allowed myself three. (These were two pairs of binoculars, one still in use, and a typewriter, which I sold for £15 despite the fact that it had German characters.) So the souvenir hunters went away empty handed.

We laid up most of the boats at Cairnryan and the rest at Lisahally on Lough Foyle in Northern Ireland. The Allied governments had agreed that Russia, America and Britain should each choose ten U-boats to keep and the rest would be towed out to sea and scuttled. For this purpose a tripartite commission of officers from the three countries was appointed to make the selection. I led the RN team and in due course we all embarked in the cruiser *Liverpool*, which provided us with accommodation during the week or so it took to make our choice. Our inspections were fairly perfunctory as the Royal Navy did not particularly want any U-boats, but the Russians were most meticulous and boarded every boat. Eventually our job was complete and we prepared to disband ourselves.

The second-in-command of the *Liverpool* was a well-known officer called Peter Dawnay.[66] His wife was the daughter of a Scottish duke whose castle was near Cairnryan. Dawnay kindly invited the leader of the Russian team, Captain Orel, another officer and me to have tea with his in-laws. All unsuspecting, Orel embarked with us in a hired car. We drove some miles before coming to a lodge house. 'What a nice house. This is where your wife's family live?' asked Orel.

'Not exactly here,' answered Dawnay. The enormous gates opened and our car advanced up the long drive. To Orel's horror we turned into the courtyard of an immense castle, complete with battlements and drawbridge. Dawnay introduced us all to the Duke and Duchess, who gave us tea and whisky on the terrace. Orel was polite but clearly uncomfortable. 'I do hope nobody in Moscow hears of this,' he said as we left. 'They don't like dukes.'

15

POST-WAR SERVICE IN THE MEDITERRANEAN FLEET (1945-48)

ADMIRALTY (SEPTEMBER 1945 – APRIL 1947)

My next job was in the Operations Division of the Admiralty which was still staffed to war standard. There were six commanders in Ops (Home), including me with an Acting 3rd stripe, all recently back from sea, and six RNVR commanders in Ops (Foreign) who seemed to be all city men. They were called Barclay, Hoare, Courage, Gabriel and other household names. They all read the *Financial Times* before starting on the day's signals, a habit which spread to Ops (Home) where we were all soon speculating like mad on the stock market. I never had any spectacular successes or failures. The only really good tip I ever received was from my brother Tony, who told me the news of the gold strike at Odendaalsrust. Unfortunately the tip came by airmail so when I placed my buying order the rise had already taken place and I got in at the top. I asked him to send me a cable the next time.

One of our commanders was a bit vague about Kaffir stocks and bought 500 West Wits at £5 when he meant to buy West Rands or some such share at 5 shillings. He was horrified when he realised his mistake and hurriedly phoned his stockbroker to sell. When he received the account he was delighted to find that in the short time he had owned the shares they had jumped several shillings and he had made a profit of £300.

I was promoted to commander in June 1946 at the age of thirty-five, which was slightly below the average. In those days you had no inkling of what your chances of promotion were each half-year and as midnight approached on 31 December and 30 June the tension was agonising. Fewer than half the lieutenant commanders received promotion during the six-year zone in which they were eligible. As each half-year slipped by the chances became less and the anxiety greater. It was rather a brutal system and many good men were 'passed over' in peacetime who later made their names in war. I was naturally delighted to make it fairly early on in the zone.

Despite rationing, and shortages of nearly everything, life in London was quite fun in these early post-war days. Once a week the Ops (Home) commanders acted as Duty Commander of the Admiralty. We were not confined to the building and could venture into the West End provided we left a telephone number and slept (perhaps 'woke up' would have been more accurate) in the Duty Commander's cabin. Other nights I commuted to Liphook.

Only once was I called on to do anything. There was a power station strike, in Cardiff I think, and on one Saturday evening the First Sea Lord sent for me and said he wanted to send two submarines to provide power for the docks. I explained that it wasn't a good idea as modern submarines produced electric power at 440V DC while the dock machinery required 220V AC. However, the admiral insisted that we always used submarines for providing power, quoting 1922 and 1930 as examples, so the submarines were duly sent. I expect they were able to provide some lighting if nothing more.

One day I was sent for by my director and told in great secrecy that my desk in Ops was required for a VIP who needed a job in London while awaiting marriage to Princess Elizabeth. (It appeared that I was the one officer in the whole Admiralty who could be most easily spared.) Lieutenant Prince Philip Mountbatten duly arrived and I commenced turning over to him my few duties. He seemed pleased that there wasn't much work to do because he said he didn't expect to spend much time in the office.

I was promised a good appointment, which turned out to be second-in-command (confusingly called commander) of the cruiser *Euryalus*, just completing refit at Rosyth. I could have asked for nothing better and in October I joined her in good spirits and in high hopes.

EURYALUS AND MOUNTBATTEN
(SEPTEMBER 1947 – JULY 1948)

Until the real captain arrived I enjoyed a couple of months of independent command. There was not much work for the CO to do, although the *Euryalus* officers and supply department were run off their feet. Routine maintenance and paperwork had been neglected for the war years so there was much tidying up to do.

Rosyth Dockyard had expanded during the war and had suffered no air raid damage, but there were still areas which had become overgrown since the great days of the Kaiser's War. Among the stacks of reserve gun barrels for classes of ships long extinct there was plenty of wildlife. I shot rabbits, hares, pigeons, duck and even pheasants. The estate of Lord Elgin was alongside, or marched with the dockyard. On Saturdays the word seemed to get around among the pheasants that the dockyard would be much safer than their usual haunts. When the guns assembled and the beaters drove, the pheasants came over the dockyard wall in fair numbers. But not to safety, for waiting for them was your author with his trusty 12-bore. Being a fairly bad game shot my bag was not great but I felt I could spare a brace for the admiral superintendent, Sir Angus Cunninghame Graham. He was not as appreciative as I had hoped. He told me I was little better than a poacher, that the pheasants belonged to Lord Elgin and furthermore that he, the admiral, was one of the regular Saturday guns.

The marvellous golf courses of Scotland were little affected by the war. Although transport was a problem, I had many enjoyable rounds at St Andrews, Muirfield, Gleneagles and even Carnoustie, of which, although a championship course, I have a low opinion. Brother Tony, over from South Africa for a brief holiday, stayed with me on board *Euryalus* and we had a day at St Andrews. We took caddies but it was soon apparent that there was something wrong with Tony's. My caddie kept putting a hand on his arm and seemed to be guiding him to the ball. We asked if he was all right, to which the reply was 'Och, the poor old chap is quite blind. But caddying is all he knows so we help him along!'

We had a visit from the US Navy Training Squadron led by the battleship *Wisconsin*. We were all asked to do what we could to entertain the officers. I volunteered an invitation to two officers to come to a guest night dinner on board the *Euryalus*, also a day's golf at St Andrews for two officers. Both were politely accepted, but for our dinner two warrant officers arrived, which was not quite what we had expected, and for the golf, neither officer nominated turned up at the landing. I received a message to say that they were a little hung-over and couldn't make it. As I had hired a car at some expense I was a bit cross. Also somewhat put out was Lord Elgin, who had invited four midshipmen to tea. He laid on a big spread, but nobody arrived. Next morning he received a letter from the US admiral thanking him for entertaining the young officers to tea, which they all said they had much enjoyed. His Lordship felt this was the final insult and immediately telephoned the American ambassador in London. I doubt if the four mids got ashore very often for the rest of the cruise.

Captain Cecil C. Hardy assumed command in December and a week later we sailed for Malta to join the 1st Cruiser Squadron which was commanded by Rear Admiral the Earl Mountbatten of Burma, who had just returned to the Navy after being Viceroy of India during the partition period.

There was still a fair-sized Mediterranean Fleet, which included our four cruisers, *Liverpool, Mauritius, Euryalus* and one other, making a good show in the Grand Harbour of Valletta. Mountbatten flew his flag in each of the ships from time to time. We had the honour quite often, and I got to know him fairly well. I was to serve with him on two further occasions.

It was impossible not to admire Mountbatten. His exceptional good looks, his outstanding war career and his mastery of the naval profession made him something of a national hero. People remarked on his great charm of manner. It is true he had this, but it was something he could switch on and off like a searchlight. It was not very often turned in my direction – to me he seemed just like any other demanding old admiral. He worked his staff extremely hard. For example, after a party (and he attended one most nights), he would settle down about midnight and dictate to his machine for an hour or so. The results had to be fair-typed and on his breakfast table at 9.00 a.m. He told me that he had to write a letter to the King once a month, which had to be in his own hand. The staff would be told to draft paragraphs for this letter which would be collated and sent for his approval. It would come back with many corrections and would then be typed fair. Finally Mountbatten would copy it out in longhand and send it off for the information of His Majesty. I often wondered if the Board of Admiralty knew about this somewhat irregular method of briefing His Majesty.

One night in Malta, in my captain's absence in hospital, I had the honour of entertaining the Admiral and Lady Edwina to dinner on board *Euryalus*. It was far from a grand affair but my chef had put his best foot forward and the creamed octopus starters and roast quail on toast tasted pretty good to me. But Mountbatten was a little bored and started tapping his finger on the table. He was not much inclined to listen but if you suggested a subject – India, America, Russia, nuclear war, polo, electronics, what you will, he would give you a fascinating five-minute briefing. He seemed to have met everybody of importance in the world and had strong views on every subject.

There was, however, a pause in the conversation at this dinner party, which I felt I had to fill. 'Sir,' I said, 'Did you ever hear the story that caused Queen Victoria to say she was not amused?' This was dangerous ground because when he felt like it Mountbatten could be *plus royaliste que le roi*. 'No, I don't think I have. What was the story?'

'Well, it seems that one night at dinner at Balmoral a young courtier thought he might enliven the rather heavy atmosphere by telling the Queen about a funny paragraph which he had noticed in a local paper. "Ma'am, do you know what they put in the *Roxburgh Gazette*?" "No, Lord Alvanly," (for it was he), "What was it they put in the *Roxburgh Gazette*?" "Ma'am, it was so funny. It said: 'The Countess of Aberdeen, on her way north to join Her Majesty at Balmoral, broke her journey at Melrose and passed the night in the Duke of Roxburghe's Arms.'" "We are not amused," said the Queen.'

Everyone looked at Mountbatten as I finished this story. 'I don't think that's very funny,' he said.

Among his other accomplishments Mountbatten was a skilful wa-terskier. One night he was to dine on board one of our cruisers and decided to make a good entrance. (Perhaps Noel Coward, who was staying with him at the time, was behind this.) The gangway staff, the bo'sun's mates, the officer of the watch, and the captain were assembled to greet him. The admiral's barge approached at full speed towing the admiral on water skis. There was nothing remarkable in this except that he was wearing full mess dress. He stepped lightly on to the bottom step of the gangway as the barge swished past without even getting his feet wet.

Euryalus gave a very grand party at Athens to which the whole royal family of Greece, all relations of Mountbatten, and most of the diplomatic corps were invited. One of the guests was a US Navy admiral called Snackenberg. When I met him he said he was thinking of calling himself Mountsnacken for the evening, but he wasn't sure if the admiral would be amused. I assured him it was quite certain that he would *not* be amused.

When the guests had left, Mountbatten shook hands with the marines who had been passing round the drinks and congratulated them. He thanked the Maltese chief steward for organising such a good party. He told the captain that the ship was looking very smart and turned to me and said 'Goodnight, Wingfield.' I felt I deserved a little more as I had organised the whole affair but my turn was to come.

Mountbatten did not have much of a sense of humour but he had a sense of fun. When Queen Frederica came to dinner on board she made him an apple-pie bed while the men were drinking their port. This was just the sort of joke he liked. When the Queen signalled her thanks for the party next morning she added, 'I hope you slept well.'

'Very well, thank you Ma'am, after certain adjustments had been made.'

If you were serving under Mountbatten it was no bad thing to play polo. I somehow acquired a rather hard-mouthed pony and played regularly when we were in Malta. Mountbatten gave me some coaching and even lent me a book on polo. 'I wrote it,' he explained, 'the year the Navy team, of which I was captain, won the Army Inter-Regimental polo tournament.'

I was not much good at polo but enjoyed what were known as Slow Chukkas. My pony had learnt a thing or two over the years and had a habit of swerving just as I was approaching the ball. One day when I missed the ball badly Mountbatten shouted, 'Get off and kick it. You're obviously not going to hit it.'

Every Sunday morning when the Squadron was in company, Mountbatten would embark in his barge and make a critical inspection of each ship. Accompanying him, armed with a telescope and signal pad, would be the commander of his flagship. 'Boat-rope in the water; metal polish spilt down side; cable not painted white; ensign not fully hoisted,' he would dictate. Once I thought he was going a bit far when he included 'Awning lacings not symmetrically arranged.' *Euryalus* usually came well out of this examination as I went round the ship half an hour before the admiral made his tour and made sure that we had no faults.

When my time in *Euryalus* came to an end Mountbatten kindly invited me to lunch just before I sailed for the UK.

'Tell me, Mervyn,' he said, 'is your captain quite mad?' I was a bit nonplussed and could hardly say 'yes' so I stammered something about him being a bit odd. Mountbatten went on, 'I have just been reading his confidential reports on the senior officers in *Euryalus*. He has marked all of them, including you, as below average. Your ship, Mervyn, has won every competition in the Fleet including the regatta, her appearance is outstanding, and she is regularly first in drills and evolutions at sea and in harbour. How can all the heads of departments be below average? I propose to exercise my rights and revise your report to read above average.'

I suppose handling a ship is like riding a horse or sailing a yacht. Some people will never do it well however much they practise. Captain Hardy was one of these. His efforts to get the ship alongside were painful to watch. He usually finished up trying to make the ship go sideways. One day we took over an hour and at least a hundred engine orders to get alongside the dockyard wall. At last the telegraphs were put to Finished with Engines. Immediately the telephone from the engine room rang. 'Chief here, Sir. Do you really mean Finished with Engines because I still have Slow Ahead Port and Half Astern Starboard to do.'

A cruiser captain should be able to do his day's work in a couple of hours in the forenoon, but not Hardy. He insisted on approving all outgoing letters, even those on technical matters. Once the surgeon commander came fuming into the wardroom saying the captain had altered a letter he had drafted to the medical director general so that it now made no sense to a doctor.

Hardy had been a specialist in Physical Training. This branch does not usually attract the brightest sparks in the Navy but presumably they have to promote one occasionally or nobody would volunteer for the branch. Hardy had been something of an athlete but had permanently crocked himself at an early age. His inability to play any game or take any exercise beyond a gentle walk probably preyed on his mind. Perhaps he tried to compensate by slaving at his desk until all hours.[67]

My time in *Euryalus* had been a pleasant experience on the whole. We cruised the Mediterranean from Gib to Alex. We had parties and sightseeing and lots of sport. It was a sporting occasion that sticks in my mind. The fleet regatta was held at Argostoli and we had a wardroom crew in the officers' race. We had spent a week at Istanbul (Constantinople) shortly before the regatta so our training had been sporadic and our physical fitness not perhaps all it should have been. I remember coming off shore at 5 a.m., taking off my mess dress, donning rowing rig and going straight off for a training row. Our crew was not much fancied for the race. The aircraft carrier had a crew of Canadian sub-lieutenants who trained exclusively on milk and were favourites. Disloyally I backed them on the Tote with a pound or two. Someone chided us on our supposedly unserious attitude to the race. I told him this was not true – we had all agreed that we would not smoke during the race.

The race day came. Our crew of six elderly officers, stroked by me aged thirty-eight, was towed to the start. My mind went back twenty years to the same regatta when *Warspite* officers, with me as bow, had won. Perhaps this inspired us for, after a desperate struggle with the Canadian subs, we won by half a length. Instead of collapsing on our oars I told the crew to keep on paddling, which we did till we reached *Euryalus*. This bit of showmanship was well received by the ships' company, who gave us a big cheer. I think many of them had backed us on the Tote, which paid out 8 to 1.

16

WASHINGTON AND PARIS
(MAY 1949 – SEPTEMBER 1950)

I enjoyed my foreign service leave at Liphook in the spring of 1949. Our children Cicely, now eight, and Richard, now six, had been joined by Peter, born in May 1948 while I was at sea in *Euryalus*. Captain Hardy, in an uncharacteristic gesture, had opened a bottle of champagne in celebration. We were just finishing the bottle when in came the engineer officer, Commander Gay, who announced that he had just become the father of a bouncing girl. 'What's the matter with this ship today?' grumbled the captain as he rang for his steward.

My next appointment was to the British Joint Services Mission in Washington, as Staff Officer with the admiral commanding US Navy submarines. This involved moving the family plus our faithful Nanny to New London, Connecticut, where I rented a roomy but old-fashioned house beside the golf course. This was a very happy time. With local allowances, my commander's pay came to the same as an American rear admiral's. I visited every submarine squadron including those as far afield as Hawaii, San Diego and

A family portrait

Key West. I spent weeks at sea in US submarines and reported on the work of many of their scientific research establishments. In the winter we moved back to Washington DC, where I was lucky enough to find another old-fashioned house in Chevy Chase. It was old-fashioned to Americans, hence its low rent, but it seemed pretty modern to us.

Life in Washington was interesting from a service point of view. We all had our US Navy contacts in the Pentagon where we spent much time. Washington was a good centre for making trips about the country and the little passenger aircraft called, I think, an Expeditor, was invaluable. Every few weeks it would take two or three of us to the West Coast or Ottawa or Key West, Florida. It was flown by Fleet Air Arm pilots attached to the Mission and it had an admirable record for safety and reliability. But this was not to last. The RAF asked to borrow it. We were assured that their pilot was highly skilled, in fact a much decorated Battle of Britain hero. He went to land at Pensacola I think, or some other airfield which was at a height of 6,000 feet, but forgot to allow for the thin air. Our dear little plane dropped out of the air at 50 feet and was never the same again.

Although we were surrounded by golf courses, not one of them would accept us at a price we could afford. One member of the Mission had rich friends and used to hunt with the Maryland every Saturday but, for most of us, cocktail parties, sometimes two or three in an evening, were the principal social activity. One weekend I took the family to Niagara Falls, where we were briefly in trouble. We walked across the Rainbow Bridge and unknowingly entered Canada. When we turned back the immigration officers treated us as illegal immigrants without papers. They pretended they had not seen us walk over the bridge a few minutes earlier. After a while they grudgingly let us enter the USA.

I believe the immigration service is very badly paid. They certainly seemed to enjoy making things difficult for visitors. I was landing at New York once and was being questioned by one of these characters. 'Have you ever been associated with any Communist organisations?' he asked. 'Oh yes,' I replied brightly, 'I was attached to the Red Fleet in North Russia in 1942.' He looked shocked so I explained the circumstances. 'Listen Mac,' he warned me, 'don't try and be funny with us.' But the Australian behind me was quick with his reply to the question, 'Why do you want to enter the United States?' 'I do *not* want to enter the US – I'd be much happier in Sydney, but your government asked me to help them out with some technical matters and that's why I'm here.'

After eighteen months with the US Submarine Force I was appointed to the Armed Forces Staff College, Norfolk, Virginia for a six-month course. This establishment was often called the Armed Forces Golf College because of its proximity to the Army Navy Golf Club. I thoroughly enjoyed its facilities, played regularly with the admiral in command and reached an American golf handicap of 9, my best ever. We had good friends living at Virginia Beach where we had many beach parties.

I summarised my impressions of US submarines in a final report to the Admiralty (Flag Officer Submarines), in which I said, inter alia, that in my judgement, after two years' observation, all the equipment in the US submarines was superior to the equivalent in British submarines and that US submarines generally were superior to our own in material efficiency. I maintain to this day that I was right at the time, but naturally my views were not well received by Flag Officer Submarines. I did not question the operational ability of British submarines vis-à-vis US submarines. Despite our inferior equipment, in this respect I think the balance lay in our favour.

Eventually, in January 1951, we packed up our belongings, including a marvellous 8-cylinder 1949 Pontiac, and sailed for home in the *Franconia*.[68] I had a good spell of foreign service leave, during which we moved from our small house in Liphook to a larger one beside the 16th fairway of Liphook golf course. 'More of a gentleman's residence,' said my father-in-law's chauffeur approvingly. (This was to be our home for the next twenty-seven years. In 1978, the children being all grown up with families of their own, we moved to a smaller house at Hindhead, where we now live. We still spend much time at Liphook, which is only ten minutes away, and I divide my golf between the two courses.)

My next appointments were with the North Atlantic Treaty Organisation (NATO), in Paris and in Norfolk, Virginia. The first was as ADC to the Naval Deputy Supreme Commander at Supreme Headquarters Allied Powers Europe (SHAPE). He was a charming French admiral who had been head of the French Navy where he had the difficult job of making a united force from the Free French and Vichy French factions. Admiral André Lemonnier was known in his own service as Le Petit Baigneur from his habit of swimming from the gangway of his last command, the battleship *Richelieu*.[69]

I found NATO jobs rather frustrating – fighting imaginary wars with armies and navies which have existence only in the War Plans Department. But there were compensations. We travelled all over Europe with General Eisenhower in his aircraft called Columbine. I trotted along behind my admiral, who trotted along behind the general. Mrs Eisenhower often accompanied the general. I remember once we were playing canasta, which she adored, as the plane approached Oslo. There was the guard of honour, the band and a knot of VIPs waiting on the tarmac to welcome the general and Mrs Eisenhower. 'Play faster!' she urged us as the plane circled. Finally she said triumphantly, 'You each owe me 25 cents.' She then returned to her cabin to put on her hat. As she emerged she asked what place this was. Oslo, she was told. 'Do I know the boss?' she asked. 'Yes, you met him once in Paris. His name is General Ole Nielsen.' Putting on a big smile she went down the gangway and embraced the Norwegian chief of staff. 'Gee, it's good to see you again, Ole. Remember that party we had in Paris?' She was a delightful person, perpetually surprised at finding herself so important. Playing bingo one night she won a pop-up toaster – she was enchanted with this success and not at all put out when Mrs Grunther, the chief of staff's wife, told her she already had six of them at home.

General Eisenhower was always considerate to his staff. Once, after a busy day, we landed at Copenhagen where we had booked the whole of the first floor of the Hotel Angleterre, as was the custom. The general called over his personal ADC, a young USAF colonel, who also piloted Columbine. 'Ed,' he said, 'the boys deserve a party. Take them all out to dinner and have a fine time. I'm going to hit the sack.'

Evidently Ed did some telephoning for when we arrived at the Tivoli Gardens, the red carpet was laid out on the steps of the restaurant and the manager, flanked by the head waiter and sommelier, showed us to the top table, which was heaped with flowers. After ordering crevettes and canard pressé à l'orange, he chose the wine. 'Two magnums of Charles Heidsieck,' he said, adding for our benefit, 'We must try to be as economical as possible. Champagne is cheaper by the magnum.' When we left, Ed signed the bill with a flourish 'D. D. Eisenhower, SHAPE, Paris'. A memorable evening.

General Eisenhower, Arromanches Beach, June 1951

We visited Normandy on one tour and I took a photograph of the general looking pensively over the D-Day beaches. At Cherbourg we saw some units of the French Navy which were flying different ensigns – some the tricolour and some the Croix de Lorraine. I asked my admiral about this and he explained that feelings still ran too high between the factions to order the Croix de Lorraine to be hauled down but he thought that it would all sort itself out in a year or two.

In early 1952 Admiral Lemonnier established the NATO Defence College in the old École Militaire in Paris. There were students of all three services from all the NATO nations with a sprinkling of diplomats, civil servants and, I suspect, CIA men. We had simultaneous translation for the lectures, which were given by distinguished national and international figures. We did long tours of Europe from Norway to Sicily and Ankara, and generally much enjoyed ourselves. As Lemonnier's aide-de-camp I became Student No. 1 on Course No. 1. The College exists to this day but has moved from one country to another several times.

When the course ended I asked Lemonnier to make out a confidential report on me for transmission to the Admiralty, as is required at the end of an appointment. He certainly turned up trumps and gave me a superb write-up in the most flowery French. I refused to have it translated as I felt that much of its flavour would be lost, so the Admiralty received it verbatim. Apparently they liked it as I was soon appointed Staff Plans Officer to the Supreme Allied Commander Atlantic, otherwise known as the US Commander-in-Chief Atlantic Fleet.

This was to be a most unenjoyable interlude. I arrived at the Norfolk, Virginia headquarters where I was allocated an office and was provided with a room in the Bachelor Officers' Quarters overlooking the golf course. This was the only good feature of my job. It started badly on my first day when a staff memo marked to all staff officers was dropped into my in-tray. It read:

'All staff officers are notified that a Royal Navy Officer has joined the Staff on an exchange basis. It is important that he should be given information only on a strict Need-to-Know basis.'

As a result, the only papers I received were 'Navy News' and the Daily Orders. I became extremely bored and complained to our admiral in Washington that I was wasting my time. However, he held the view that it was my fault and suspected that I was trying to wangle an appointment at home. This was quite untrue. All I wanted was a job to do. I had bought a beautiful new Pontiac and would have been happy to stay in the USA. After a few months a relief for me was appointed, and I was told, rather insultingly, that I was not to meet him (in case I contaminated him, I suppose). I was pleased to see a month or two later that the appointment had been abolished, my successor having received the same treatment as I had and made the same complaints.

During this period I found that if I took a long lunch hour and drifted back to the office around 2.30, I encountered dark looks from the chief of staff. However, if I didn't come back at all in the afternoon nobody noticed. This enabled me to play golf most afternoons, often, oddly enough, with the commander-in-chief himself. We played for modest stakes by American standards but I once found myself faced with a 6 foot putt for $50 which, of course, I holed! (So memory tells me, but as in all forms of gambling one forgets the misses.)

I sold my Pontiac at a loss of $1,000, which hurt a bit. The buyer was a Methodist parson. When I complained about the low price he was offering he reminded me that I didn't have much choice as he knew I was sailing on the *Queen Elizabeth* on Thursday.

The voyage, my fourth in a Cunarder, was great fun. I made the acquaintance of Miss Ginger Rogers, who had been a top star so long that she had lost any grand ideas. We danced and drank champagne, Charles Heidsieck, of course – in fact on the last night of the voyage we drank the Verandah Grill dry of this brand. When she landed the press asked her about her voyage. 'Very quiet,' she said. 'I spent most of the time in my cabin reading Shakespeare.'

Once I introduced her to Sir Robert Watson-Watt, the inventor of radar. 'Oh, Sir Robert,' she said, 'do tell me all about radar.' He did his best and described the early days of the art which I, at least, found most interesting. Ginger contrived to look interested and gave him a thank-you kiss.

Another time I was having a drink with a quiet American couple when a large, fat Texan started becoming rather noisy at the end of the bar. My companion made some remark about how he couldn't stand Texan millionaires, which the fat man heard. He lurched over and demanded to know what was wrong with Texan millionaires. Somehow he was soothed and after he left we went in to dinner. I had not identified my companion, so I introduced myself and asked him his name. 'John D. Rockefeller III,' he said.

Back at the Admiralty I went to see the vice chief of the naval staff, Sir Rhoderick McGrigor, who, unlike our admiral in Washington, was most sympathetic. He had read my reports and agreed that I had been put in an impossible position. He said he would give me a job in Plans Division where he would keep his eye on me. This he did to such good effect that on 30 June 1953 I was promoted captain.

17

THE GARE LOCH, SCOTLAND
(JULY 1954 – MAY 1955)

The rank of captain, or post captain as it used to be called, is by far the best in the Navy. There are a great variety of interesting jobs available. There is security for nine and a half years, at the end of which you become either a rear admiral or a captain (retired). In your last year you are appointed an extra ADC to the Queen which allows you to wear aiguillettes on the right shoulder and add ADC to any other letters which you may already have after your name.

Anyway, thus started the last phase of my naval career, which commenced with the Senior Officers' Technical Course, a leisurely affair spent touring the research establishments in considerable comfort. I was keen to have the Admiralty spend as much money as possible on my professional education, so I was pleased to add the Senior Officers' Technical Course to the Naval Staff College Greenwich, the École Militaire (NATO Defence College) and the US Armed Forces Staff College. Later I was to add the Senior Officers' War Course.

After the Senior Officers' Technical Course I joined HMS *Jupiter* in January 1954 as Senior Officer Reserve Fleet Clyde and Resident Naval Officer, West of Scotland. The whole family moved to the Helensburgh area where, after moving twice, we settled in a Scottish mansion called Cragmhor on a hillside overlooking the Gare Loch near Rhu. I also had a depot ship, HMS *Woolwich*, which was duty-free, surprisingly, despite the fact that we never went to sea. With an ample staff of cooks and stewards, gardeners, a coxswain and two chauffeurs we lived pretty

Sheila adding the rum, Christmas 1955, HMS Jupiter

With Sheila and Betsy

well. (The reason for two chauffeurs is that when I had only one, she said she was overworked by our going out to frequent dinners and other evening functions and she didn't get enough sleep. So I had a day and a night chauffeur, both of whom were Wrens.) We entertained both ashore and afloat, but I always maintained that my parties on board *Woolwich* were the best.

My wife, having been brought up in a large house called Glenfinart at Ardentinny on nearby Loch Long, had a family acquaintance with various local landowners who included a whisky baron and a shipping magnate, so our social life in Scotland started with an advantage.

The ships in reserve were mostly in the Gare Loch, where the battleships *Howe* and *King George V*, an aircraft carrier, several cruisers and half a dozen miscellaneous vessels were moored. At Greenock there were twenty or thirty landing ships and at Rosyth a batch of destroyers, frigates and corvettes. It was quite a large command, although most of the ships needed little maintenance as they were destined for the scrapyard. This was not the case for the landing ships, however, which were kept in good condition. This was amply proved at the time of the Suez emergency when all of them were hurriedly commissioned and did good service in that disappointing operation.

The Home Fleet paid a visit to the Clyde and I was invited to dine with the commander-in-chief. To enliven the conversation I remarked to the C.-in-C. that my fleet was considerably larger than his. He gave me a cold look but made no reply. Bang went another rung in my promotional ladder.

The ratings, being mostly townsmen, considered a drafting to Scotland as a disagreeable form of foreign service, but most of the officers enjoyed the open-air pursuits which Scotland provides in such abundance. In one week I sailed a dinghy in Clyde Week regatta and won a second prize; played a golf match at Gleneagles; shot grouse on the Reserve Fleet's private moor and stalked a stag on Ben Lomond. A pleasantly balanced life. Anything you do in Scotland can be done in the rain.

I was lucky to have a most genial admiral, Geoff Robson, at Rosyth. He was my overlord in all local matters, excluding ships, which came under the Admiral Commanding Reserves. I often stayed at Admiralty House, Rosyth where Admiral Robson entertained on a grand scale. I remember once finding to my horror that my steward had failed to pack my dinner jacket. I appealed to the admiral's valet for help. 'No trouble, Sir,' he said. 'The admiral has three dinner jackets and you are just his size.' Apparently I got away with it as the admiral did not recognise his own jacket.[70]

Unfortunately Admiral Robson was deaf in one ear, due to gunfire. At lunch one day Lady Mountbatten made vain attempts to make conversation. Finally she turned angrily away from him and towards me, sitting on her right. 'The man's as deaf as a post,' she said. 'I'm going to talk to you.' I had a fascinating half-hour of Edwina Mountbatten's views on everything under the sun. She had recently been to stay with an old friend, Pandit Nehru, at her old residence, the viceregal lodge at Delhi. I asked her what it was like under the new regime. 'Mervyn,' she said, 'the water flowed like champagne.'

While her husband, who was First Sea Lord, was inspecting all the various naval activities in Scotland, Edwina did her bit by addressing meetings of all the senior officers' wives. Her theme was that they spent too much time giving cocktail parties for each other and did not do enough for the ratings. When my wife reported this to me I said, 'Right, we will give a cocktail party at our official house for all the senior ratings,' which we did, adding all the heads of departments to help us out. Eight or ten chief petty officers turned up with their wives who promptly sat down on all the sofas and armchairs and refused to circulate.

Our staff plied them with brandy and ginger ale, 'horses' necks', (nowadays it has replaced gin as the Navy's favourite drink), but nothing would stir them. The CPOs mixed easily with the commanders, but not so their wives. My wife struggled valiantly but I had to agree with my steward who after everything was over said, 'Not one of our most successful parties, Sir.'

This same petty officer steward became quite a friend and served us faithfully for two years. I trusted him implicitly and let him do all the catering. When he left for a new posting I felt a considerable loss.

This was enhanced when bills started coming in from the butcher, the grocer and the baker. Apparently he had not paid any of my accounts for the last two months. I traced him to his new appointment which was in the Royal Yacht *Britannia*, where he was Prince Philip's valet. He said he would send me a cheque for the amount outstanding in a couple of months and expressed his regret for forgetting to pay the bills. Sure enough the cheque turned up in due course and all was well, but I wondered how he raised the money.

Our CPO cook was a real 'treasure', as they used to say. He was brilliant at his job and his dishes not only looked good but tasted good too, which is not always the case with Service chefs. Once I was giving a dinner on board where the high point of the meal was a giant soufflé. Just at the crucial moment a junior electrical engineer stopped the generator for some reason and all the lights and power, including the chef's cooker, went off. The chef was furious and roundly abused the officer for spoiling the captain's dinner. The officer put him on a charge of behaving with disrespect and in due course he appeared before me, much to my embarrassment. Although I fully sympathised, discipline had to be preserved. I sentenced the chef to be 'Reprimanded' but I gave the officer a proper dressing down for his stupidity. 'Electrical officers are two a penny,' I told him, 'but first-class chefs are hard to find.'

I was at one of these dinners that I had Ronald Teacher as a guest.[71] For some reason I remember the menu. It was:

Escargots

Roast hare

Ice cream with hot Curaçao

Haggis with whisky sauce

I asked Ronald, who was a good friend, what he would like to drink. 'Anything you like, Mervyn. Sherry, beer or champagne, anything except Teacher's Highland Cream.' He told me how he had inherited a small and very localised business from his father at the age of twenty-five. He had built it up from a distillery and six pubs in Glasgow to an international organisation capitalised at many million pounds. 'You have to drink a hell of a lot of Highland Cream to become a market leader in the USA, South America and Australia, as well as in the UK. I did that in ten years.'

He also told me his unusual financial problem. He and his wife, sadly, had no children so what was he to do with his money? He was bound to leave several million but what was the point of leaving it to his nephews, who were all in the whisky business and wouldn't notice an extra half million or so if he gave it to them. I muttered something about youth clubs but he said he was already financing several.

He had a beautiful yacht called *Mariella* with four paid hands, which was often the committee boat at local regattas. Although he had been Dragon class champion in his youth, in his later years he did not often put the sails up. When he did it was said the moths flew out.

Ronald gave me my first introduction to grouse shooting. His moor overlooking the Clyde was famous and his shoots were highly organised. Twenty beaters, four keepers. Two drives before lunch and two after. Hot steak and kidney pie and lashings of whisky. I was not a good shot by these standards but I did not do too badly.

Ronald also invited me to a pheasant shoot. It was January and the orders were, 'Cocks only. Ten shillings to the head keeper for anyone who shoots a hen.' At the pick-up there was one hen, which regrettably was marked up against me. But this was not all. The head keeper held up an owl. 'Which of the gentlemen shot this, may I ask?' Of course it was me.

In our Reserve Fleet there was a young lieutenant who was extremely keen on shooting and also owned a well trained gun dog. Tom Gullick suggested that we might try to restore and re-stock Rosneath moor, which was within my 'parish'. It had once been a well known moor. In about 1905 an article in the *Sporting and Dramatic* featured my father-in-law, Major Leschallas, showing a record bag of grouse. But the area had been occupied by the American Army in the 1940s and they had destroyed everything that flew, ran or crawled. However, the remains of the butts were there and Gullick worked hard at building them up again.

In the Reserve Fleet there was an official rat-catcher, who had apparently caught all the rats and so had little to do. I asked him what his job had been before he joined the civil service. 'I was second keeper on Lord Roseberry's estate at Dalmeny,' he told me. 'Right,' I said, 'get up to the moor and clear out all the vermin, hooded crows, stoats, etc.'

All grouse want is heather (which should not be too high), water and gravel. If the altitude is three or four hundred feet, that is even better. Rosneath had all these requirements and when the vermin were exterminated they soon came back. In my first year we shot about 100 and the second year over 200. The magazine *Scottish Field* was complimentary about our efforts and published pictures of our amateur-run grouse moor. What was even better was that I invited all the local lairds to my shoot and they invited me back to their, much superior, shoots.

One of my *ex officio* jobs was Branch Captain of the Royal Naval Sailing Association. My aversion to sailing, engendered by the Dartmouth experiences, had diminished, so I was able to take up this duty with some pleasure.

But as Captain of Royal Navy Golf (Scotland) I was in my element. We had a good programme of team matches on courses all over southern Scotland. We got to know all the courses on the Ayrshire coast, as well as the Fifeshire ones, Gleneagles and Pitfirrane. Our local course at Helensburgh is unknown in the golfing world, but if you put it down in the middle of Texas it would cost you $10,000 to join. I suppose there are about 100 courses around Glasgow, most of them near top class, but few people seem to have heard of them.

If all this suggests that life at Faslane on the Gare Loch (now the nuclear submarine base of the Royal Navy) was all sports and parties, I have to admit that there is some truth in the allegation. Everybody was very kind to us when my time came to an end. I was made an Honorary Member of the Royal Northern Yacht Club, principally because I was always prepared to move a battleship or a cruiser to clear the yacht racing course. The RNVR Club Glasgow gave me the same honour and the PLRs (Prominent Local Residents) gave us some excellent farewell parties.

My next appointment was as Naval Attaché, Athens (which later extended to Tel Aviv), where I and the family arrived in January 1956.

18

GREECE (JANUARY 1956 – AUGUST 1957)

Before leaving for Athens I had an interview with Admiral Mountbatten, First Sea Lord. Most of this was taken up with an explanation of his relationship with the various members of the Greek royal family. 'The King,' he said, 'is my second cousin. The Queen is also my second cousin, but through a different line.' He called my attention to an immense wall chart showing all his ancestors and collaterals, including his sisters, the Queen of Sweden and Princess Andrew of Greece.

I had eaten oysters at lunch, one of which must have been bad, for I was feeling extremely ill. As a result I may have got some of the relationships wrong. He gave me a message for the King – 'My respects'. For the Queen – 'My regards'. For Princess Andrew – 'My love.' For Prince Constantine – 'My best wishes.' I am pleased to say that I delivered all these messages in person within a month of my arrival in Athens. Princess Andrew was delighted. 'Dear Dickie,' she said, 'isn't it marvellous he has been made an Admiral of the Fleet. His father was one of those, you know, and Dickie did so want to follow in his footsteps.'

Greece is a beautiful country but all was not lovely in the garden in 1956. It was the height of the EOKA campaign and General Grivas was leading a full-scale rebellion in Cyprus, fully supported by not only the Greek government, but by Archbishop Makarios, temporarily in exile in the Seychelles. There was a total boycott of the British and my relations with the Greek Navy were cold and formal. We had no Greek friends during all the time I was there, although the King and Queen went out of their way to be nice to us on the occasions we met. This annoyed the Greek admirals.

Once there was an earthquake and I offered a Royal Navy ship to help with relief. The Navy had carried out this duty on many occasions all over the world. My offer was indignantly refused. 'We are quite capable of handling our own earthquakes without British interference,' said Admiral Lappas, chief of the naval staff.

When Britain hanged two terrorists in Cyprus for an atrocity, the mayor of Athens retaliated by renaming the street in which the British Embassy stands after them. The ambassador's beautiful Rolls-Royce had 'EOKA' scratched on all four doors and even our own car was damaged. At that time Austin cars had the words 'Austin of England' on the rear. The word 'England' was chipped off most cars of that make in Athens.

Our failure to capture Grivas and thus end the troubles in Cyprus seemed hard to explain. Time and time again our troops found his hideout with the embers of the campfire still warm, but always the bird had flown. It was not for some years that it was revealed that the governor's trusted chief of intelligence, an Anglo-Greek, was a traitor. Every anti-terrorist operation planned by the British was promptly reported to Grivas, who became a Greek hero by his ability to evade the British troops.

When Makarios was released from exile he made a triumphal entry into Athens. A motorcade, led by an open white Cadillac from which he distributed blessings, proceeded amid cheering crowds from the airport to the Grande Bretagne Hotel. There he addressed the multitude from a balcony, likening his arrival to that of our Lord's entry into Jerusalem. It was, appropriately, Palm Sunday. This odious character, with the Bible in one hand and a bomb under his cassock, stayed at the Grande Bretagne for four weeks. When he left (so the barman told me later), he blessed the chambermaid, blessed the head waiter and blessed the commissionaire, but did not leave a tip for anyone. He had once been married, but in the Greek church bishops have to be single, so he divorced his wife as soon as his preferment seemed possible.

Like most Orthodox bishops he soon became immensely rich from the drachmas contributed by the pious peasants of his diocese. After leaving the Grande Bretagne he took a house nearly opposite us in the Athens suburb of Psychiko and many a time I had to dodge smartly to avoid being blessed when we met in the street.

The Suez operation took place during our time in Athens and very exciting it was during the early stages. Like the Dardanelles landings forty years earlier, there was little secrecy about our intentions. Nevertheless the initial assault on Port Said went well and the Egyptian army were soon in full retreat. The Israelis also attacked Egypt at the same time and, despite our Prime Minister's denial, it is impossible to believe that the two operations were not co-ordinated, and quite rightly too.

I telephoned my colleague, the French naval attaché, when the news came through of our early successes and we mutually congratulated each other on what appeared to be a splendid victory for the Anglo-French forces. Then I rang the American attaché expecting his reaction to be similar. I was shocked when he said, 'Wait a minute Merv, I don't think we're on the same side.' Sure enough, the USA condemned our actions and told us we must halt our troops or all economic aid to Britain would be cut off. Anthony Eden completely lost his nerve and gave in, stopping our leading divisions when almost within sight of Suez. Some time later I met General Stockwell, the force commander, and asked him why he did not 'do a Nelson' and turn a blind eye to his orders. He said he had done just that to the first two orders but when the third came it was a personal message from the Prime Minister, which for him to ignore would have been mutiny. He said it was the most disappointing moment of his life. Total victory was in his grasp, within days or hours, when it was plucked from him.

Various factions contributed to this debacle. The US Secretary of State, John Foster Dulles, whose threats made Eden quail, could not bear the thought of success by British arms, although later he said he was surprised that Eden gave in. If we had disregarded him and had a quick victory, America would soon have come to terms with the new situation.

Then there was the attitude of the Labour Party, who fiercely opposed the operation and made a great fuss in the House of Commons about our supposed iniquity. The BBC also carries as much responsibility since their news bulletins gave an excessive amount of time to criticisms of our action, which were not well received by the troops. But most of all it was Eden's failure to support the action he had initiated. He was not a strong character and was ill and suffering from lack of sleep. It is impossible to imagine Churchill showing such pusillanimity.

While in Athens, I was also accredited to our embassy in Tel Aviv, Israel and was able to see something of that remarkable country, as well as meeting some of the leading people, whom I much admired. I had tea with Mrs Golda Meyer, the Foreign Minister, and enjoyed her fund of Jewish stories. One I remember concerned the visit of an Israeli frigate to Plymouth. Two of the crew, resplendent in their best uniforms, went into a pub near the docks and found themselves sharing a table with a three-badge British Able Seaman. He eyed them as they drank their pints. 'What Navy are you from then?' he asked. 'We are Israeli Navy,' was the reply, 'Perhaps you know it better as Palestine.' 'Oh, Palestine,' replied the AB, 'We all know about Palestine. Here, you still having trouble with them Jews?'

I also met the chief of staff of the Navy, who was set on acquiring submarines for his fleet. I did my best to persuade him not to, but he was adamant. Egypt had submarines therefore he must have them. I pointed out that a submarine is not the best answer to another submarine. What he needed were half a dozen fast anti-submarine patrol craft, such as Vospers built for many foreign navies. He was not impressed and went ahead with the purchase of four second-hand British S-class submarines. One by one these came to grief by explosion, collision or just failing to surface, although I believe one survived for several years.

I did not meet Moshe Dayan, famous for the black patch over his left eye, but I did have a chat with his second-in-command. He too was full of anecdotes, mostly to the credit of his boss. After the Six Day War, Dayan ordered the vehicles and tanks of the Israeli army to be painted the same colour as the Egyptians. 'Pure economics,' he said.

'We have captured twice as many Egyptian vehicles as we had of our own, so it's cheaper to paint ours to match theirs.' When asked if he would make any changes if he had to fight the Egyptians again he said next time he would put the whole thing in his wife's name.

I remember one enjoyable picnic on the Sea of Galilee with the military attaché and his family. We found a suitable beach near a village which turned out to be named Canaa. Memories of the First Miracle came to mind and it was with mounting excitement that we unpacked the lunch basket. I uncorked the lime juice, poured some and sipped it hopefully. No luck, it was still plain lime juice.

One of the pleasant perks of the job of naval attaché is that he is allowed to visit the naval attachés of neighbouring countries once a year. Thus I had pleasant stays with my opposite numbers in Rome, Belgrade and Ankara. I also visited Cyprus where the redoubtable Tony Miers VC was in naval command.[72] My aged Aunt Olive, after many years as a missionary in China, had had to leave that country when her husband was murdered by the Communists. It was pleasant to meet her at Famagusta in Cyprus where she was running a mission for the soldiers. I asked her if she ever had any trouble, but she firmly rejected the suggestion. With her commanding presence I was not surprised. As we had tea at a beach café she asked me why I was not carrying a pistol. I told her I had one in my briefcase. 'Put it on the table,' she ordered, 'so everyone can see it. It's not the slightest good in your bag if we are attacked.'

One final memory of Athens is of a party given for the Russian naval attaché, where we hoped to get valuable information from him when he was in his cups. We had a microphone hidden in the flowers and a tape recorder in the kitchen. Egged on by our resident MI6 man, who spoke Russian, we plied Captain Ivanov with whisky, wine and vodka. Later, when we came to play the tapes, we could recognise our own voices becoming louder and louder. We even sang songs in Russian. But strangely, the soft voice of the Russian captain was almost inaudible and certainly betrayed no secrets.

The Athens Embassy, under its distinguished ambassador Sir Charles Peake MC, GCMG, had a slightly dated air. Sir Charles, who was the epitome of an old school diplomat, loved to entertain at lunchtime when we were all assembled in the drawing room. We could meet all sorts of interesting people. I remember the Duke of Kent, Clare Booth Luce, Lord Halifax, and several well-known MPs, but very few Greeks.

One day Lord Halifax, who had held every high office of state except prime minister, called me aside and asked me about my job. I told him the situation, how I was boycotted by the Greek Navy because of the EOKA campaign. 'Not much point in your being here, is there?' he said. I suggested that at least I was keeping the seat warm for my successor, which he agreed without much enthusiasm. In fact, after peace in Cyprus, relations with the Greek Navy quickly returned to the usual cordial level. As Sir Charles once said, speaking of diplomacy in general, 'Sometimes they hate you, sometimes they love you. Never let them get you down, but never let them get you *up*.'

The ambassador gave a very grand dinner for some visiting dignitary that is worth recording. The dining table was laid with Halifax family gold plate, on loan to His Excellency. No silver, nothing but gold. There were six footmen and a butler. A string orchestra played during dinner, giving place to a piper when we danced Scottish reels after the meal. We all wore full dress with orders and decorations, several of the embassy ladies surprising us with MVO or MBE badges on their dresses. Our naval full dress had recently been abolished but His Excellency insisted that I wear mine. 'I am the Queen's representative,' he said, 'and I authorise you to wear it.' His Excellency was a resplendent figure, his coat covered with gold lace set off by the brilliant sash of the Grand Cross of St Michael and St George.

Near me at this dinner was the Athens correspondent of the *New York Times*. After the fish course, he lit a cigarette, which caused Lady Peake to eye him rather coldly. 'Have a cigarette by all means,' she said sweetly, 'if you think it will improve the dinner.' The correspondent muttered an apology and stubbed his cigarette out on a gold plate which was hastily removed by a footman.

The portrait of Byron in Greek national dress looked down approvingly on our revels. One of the embassy guards told me next day what a brilliant picture we had made dancing to the bagpipes in all our finery. He had telephoned his wife to come quickly to the embassy and watch, as she might never see such a sight again.

My time in Athens was slightly shorter than I had expected. I was told, unofficially, the reason for this when I was debriefed at the Naval Intelligence Division in the Admiralty. Apparently my reports from Tel Aviv were too pro-Israeli and had upset some Arab-lovers in Whitehall. The word went out that as I appeared to have become completely Zionised it was time to recall me.

So in August 1957 I returned to England, driving a Pontiac (my third) from Athens to Calais in three days. I had intended to save money by camping, but the first evening when I pitched my tent the mosquitoes came down in myriads, making it impossible to stay there. I drove on to Graz, where I got a room at the first hotel that I came to. Its name I think was the Schwei and I was told later that it had the reputation of being the most expensive in Austria. So much for economy.

It was good to get back to Liphook and some golf again. (There was none in Greece at that time.) My next appointment, rather a disappointment, was to the Admiralty as Director of Underwater Weapons. I had no hope of a sea appointment, having been put on the General (or Dry) List, possibly on the grounds that I had had command for several years and it was time for others to have a turn. They told me I was eligible for any job in the Navy except seagoing command. I said I would quite like to command Haslar Naval Hospital. 'Sorry, that's reserved for doctors.' 'How about command of the RN Engineering College at Manadon?' 'Sorry, that's reserved for engineers.' 'The Supply and Secretariat School at Chatham?' 'Sorry, that's reserved for paymasters.'

19

ADMIRALTY AGAIN AND SCOTLAND
(1957-62)

As it turned out I quite enjoyed my three years in the Weapons Department. My boss was a splendid character called Mike Le Fanu, who soon became First Sea Lord and was nominated for Chief of the Defence Staff when he died of leukaemia.[73] He was more than somewhat eccentric and although distinguished in the Gunnery world, he was far from typical of specialists of that ilk. When in command of a ship he had the habit of dressing up in a leading seaman's uniform and mixing incognito, or so he thought, with the ratings on shore. This must be a dangerous practice, but he got away with it. It is perhaps just as well that other admirals did not imitate him or discipline would have been impaired.

I had much to do with civil servants, with whom I got on well, particularly the Admiralty ones, who I would say were the pick of the bunch. Several scientific establishments were under my umbrella and it was the job of the naval staff to keep the scientists working on sensible projects which were capable of being developed. The temptation was strong for the clever ones to go off into pure science rather than sticking with applied research.

I had one disloyal and indeed disobedient chief scientist. I did my utmost to get him moved but with no success. When his turn came for a CBE, I was asked to write the citation. This I refused to do and I made the point that he should *not* receive the award. But in the next Honours List there was his name, 'for distinguished services to naval scientific research'.

Mountbatten of Burma, 22nd June 1961

One of our priorities at this time was the development of a new torpedo to be fitted in the nuclear submarines. We had several but none of them were successful. It seemed as if 'finality in design' had been reached in the torpedo field. Some successes were, however, achieved in anti-submarine detection methods. We pushed out the range of detection to many thousands of yards. In this, as in other areas, there was no shortage of bright ideas but sonar (formerly Asdic) still showed the best results. Some of the suggestions, like training porpoises to follow enemy submarines, were so bizarre that one scientist produced a witty monograph entitled 'Unsound methods of submarine detection'.

In February 1961, having completed three months at the Senior Officers' War College, I was appointed to the Royal Naval Air Station, Abbotsinch, as commanding officer. It was a 'stone frigate', but at least it was command. The RAF professed themselves shocked at the idea of a non-aviator commanding an air station, but the Admiralty did not hold with any restrictive practices. Anybody can do anything was their motto.

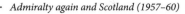

In the event all went well. In my eighteen months in command we had no major accidents and nobody was injured or killed. My predecessor had been a meticulous man who insisted on personally passing all outgoing signals and correspondence. It was useless for me to do this as I could not understand any of the technical stuff relating to aircraft modifications. I told the heads of departments not to consult me on purely aeronautical matters, for which they were much relieved. However, I did say that if they let me down once they would be reprimanded and if it happened twice they would be sacked. No difficulties of any kind resulted from this policy, which had the added advantage of enabling me to play golf most afternoons.

Royal Naval Air Station Abbotsinch was taken over by the civil airports authority just after I left and became Glasgow Airport, but in my day it was a Reserve Aircraft Station where many old planes were laid up. We had quite a bit of flying activity, however, which kept us interested. The amount of hardware lying about was a temptation to some people and resulted in my having to charge my master-at-arms with theft of naval stores. Any naval reader will appreciate the enormity of this. To have to prosecute at a court martial the senior man on the lower deck, the head of the regulating staff and the captain's confidential advisor on disciplinary matters, was a disagreeable task. At the time Scotland was a paradise for those wishing to dispose of stolen goods, using a process known as 'resetting'. If stolen goods were displayed for a period of seven days and not claimed, they became the legal property of the resetter. In my previous job at Faslane the Reserve Fleet ships had suffered badly from this legal arrangement. Anything in brass was particularly valuable and we lost a lot of scuttle clips and gangway stanchions. They even took the spare main engine bearings out of the engine room in one reserve destroyer. The police took little interest in crimes of this sort because convictions under the existing law were almost impossible to obtain.

Another court martial was on an officer who was charged and convicted of homosexual activities with ratings. There was an embarrassing moment when the principal witness suddenly declined to give evidence and withdrew all his allegations. Fortunately there was ample other evidence. The officer was sent to Barlinnie gaol for six months. Near the end of his sentence he wrote to me personally asking for a character reference which would help him get a job when he was released. My reply took a certain amount of careful wording.

Life was not all court martials but we did have one other which was of some interest. A senior chief petty officer, president of the CPO's mess, was charged with various acts of dishonesty in connection with mess funds. As is the custom in the Navy, an officer with some legal qualifications, known as the Deputy Judge Advocate, was sent up to Abbotsinch to assist me in preparing the case for the prosecution. With the authority of the Flag Officer (Air) he suggested the charges which should be brought and what lines of cross-examination we should pursue, vetoing most of my ideas as unsuitable or impracticable. The court duly assembled and on the morning of the day the DJA informed me that he was appearing as Prisoner's Friend (counsel for the defence) at the trial. I was dumbfounded at what seemed to me an act of perfidy but there was nothing I could do.

The accused was found guilty of some of the charges and sentenced to disrating. He was also ordered to make restitution of the money which he had fraudulently converted to his own use. The sentence was much less severe that I would have wished but the prosecution's case suffered from the bad advice of the DJA.

Two months later I was astonished to receive a notification from the Admiralty remarking on certain unsatisfactory features of the trial. They directed that the sentence of the court be annulled, that the accused be restored to his rank and that the money he had paid in restitution should be returned to him. There is no arguing with Their Lordships. I had to accept the decision but it was a bitter pill to swallow. I expect the DJA is now pursuing a lucrative career at the Bar.

One year to the day before I was due for retirement, I received from Their Lordships the famous 'blue letter'. To paraphrase its wording, it said that all ten members of my batch of captains were very eligible for promotion to rear admiral, all of them with distinguished careers, but unfortunately there were only three vacancies in the Flag List and I was not one of those selected. In fact I should start looking around for civilian employment. It was a beautifully worded letter with all the marks of years of 'staff polish' but the message was clear. Nor was it a surprise. I felt not the slightest bit of resentment; I was grateful to the Navy for giving me such a happy life and pleased that I had achieved a moderate success.

My last days in the Navy were quite emotional. The wardroom mess gave me a farewell dinner at which the commander presented me with an album of photographs inscribed 'Captain Wingfield, This is Your Life'. All in the best Eamonn Andrews tradition. On my last day my aircraft was escorted to the Scottish border by some of the airworthy aircraft on the station, who made graceful wing movements to say goodbye. There followed lunch with my admiral at Lee-on-Solent, nice speeches and then a big car took me back to Fair Winds, Liphook, Hampshire, just thirty-eight years after I had first donned naval uniform.

20

RETIREMENT OF A SORT

'Retirement' has a connotation of deck chairs in the sun, long evenings with the telly and a little gentle grass-mowing, punctuated by short visits to the local. I felt I was a bit too young to put my feet up completely so I looked around for a job. I got one, and have since held half a dozen others, each one being different from the last.

I have worked in a charitable organisation (until I began to enquire too closely into the finances); I have been chairman of an oil supply company (till it folded – luckily I got my money back); I have been chairman of an insurance agency, for which I foolishly gave my name as a joint and several guarantor of the overdraft. When we had to go into liquidation due to embezzlement by the managing director, I found out that all the other guarantors were 'men of straw'. I paid off all the creditors but it cleared me out. I was an assistant bursar of a big school for six months which taught me a bit about accountancy. Then I had a spell as a blind and curtain rail erector with a furniture firm in Petersfield.

But I had one steady job for nine years as Marine Manager, United Dominions Trust. My concern was to provide finance (that is, lend money) to people of good credit for the purpose of buying yachts. It was possible at that time to take out a Maritime Mortgage Loan secured on the hull of the boat. The interest charges, as in the case of house mortgage loans, were deductible for tax purposes. This was of course immensely popular with the larger taxpayers. When I joined

UDT their marine business totalled about £90,000 per annum. By a good advertising campaign and a lot of legwork, I managed to raise this to £2.75 million in my last year. When the government cancelled the tax concession in 1971 the business collapsed overnight. There was no point in keeping on a Marine Department so I resigned.

During the years with UDT I travelled the length and breadth of the land. I suppose I visited 90 per cent of all the boat builders in the UK and there can be few yacht clubs where I did not call.

Naturally one got to know most of the leading figures in yachting and when the Boat Show came on at Earls Court in January we would entertain the 'top 200' to roast beef, Beaujolais and Stilton in our hospitality room every day. There were five companies competing in the marine finance field, but we were friendly rivals. There was plenty of business for everyone. Sometimes it was nice to look around Cowes Harbour and count up the yachts that belonged to UDT.

We needed a hostess for our stand at the Boat Show. The typist supplied by head office was hopeless so we went to an agency specialising in Australian girls, who sent along a big, long-legged blonde who had no fear of admirals or earls. She and her successors for many years did a marvellous job. One of her duties was to get the names of all our guests in the visitors' book. 'May I have your name, Sir?' she asked one important-looking guest. 'My name is Strathspey – Lord Strathspey,' was the reply. 'Strathspey?' she said unbelievingly, 'I thought that was a dance.'

After leaving UDT I was at a loose end so I decided I might as well make use of my ship Master's certificate. I soon found a job as second mate on a Fyffes banana boat. This turned out badly, principally because of the captain's hatred of the Royal Navy, which was vented on me. I had made it plain to head office that my astro-navigation was very rusty but they said it didn't matter as the other mates could all take star sights. The captain, known as 'Niggling Nigel' to the crew, told me within an hour of my arrival to prepare the books for the monthly pay. He insisted that I must not ask the purser for help. Of course I had no idea of the complexities of PAYE, allotments and stoppages. Soon afterwards he told me to work out the distance from Panama to St John's, Newfoundland. This I could do as there is a book called *Ocean Passages of the World*, but when I brought him the answer he said he didn't trust the book and I must work it out from first principles. Although I suppose I had learnt how to do this forty years before, I had to admit defeat. This sort of thing went on all the time and so I was glad to leave after a month. The captain much enjoyed sacking me.

Next I joined a small timber ship trading to the Northern Baltic, as second mate. This was a happy ship and I enjoyed the work. Five hours on watch and five hours off is the rule in coasters. When you have eaten and slept there is not much time left over. I brought a sextant with me but this was considered a joke. With the Decca Chains covering the whole of the North Sea and Baltic there is no need for any other form of navigation nowadays.

We got into ice up in the Gulf of Bothnia and we had to have an ice-breaker to prevent us getting frozen in. It was a typical village in Arctic Sweden. Just the timber store, a church, a school, a filling station and a pornographic bookshop.

The chief engineer told me how he supplemented his wages. 'Listen Second, we don't get paid much so we've got to look after ourselves. In England I buy £5 worth of Rizla cigarette papers. These are illegal in Sweden so I get a good price for them from one of the dockers. Now I go to this shop and buy a dozen books of real hard porn for a couple of quid each. I don't read them, of course – they're pretty disgusting, but I have no trouble selling them in Middlesbrough or South Shields for £10 each. You want to try it, Second – it works a treat.'

My next ship was a collier carrying Australian coal from Amsterdam to Shoreham power station. This was hard work as we went through the Dover Strait about six times a month. With twenty or thirty ships on the radar scan all going in different directions, the officer of the watch has to have his wits about him. Then there are the 'bandits', ships which ignore the recommended routes – not all of them foreigners.

I remember one of the crew seemed puzzled by my presence on board. 'Is it right you was in the Navy, Second?' he asked. I admitted

I had done a few years in naval uniform. 'I expect you had a bit of trouble, did you? That's why most of us are at sea.' My stock went up tremendously with the crew, who were convinced I had been thrown out of the Navy for some dreadful crime.

A very pleasant experience in 1972 was taking a large motor yacht from Southampton to Monte Carlo via Corunna, Gibraltar, Palma and St Tropez. We fairly belted along and did the trip in thirteen days. At St Tropez we were having lunch at a dockside restaurant when I detected something vaguely familiar about the face of the lady at the next table. She was good-looking but clearly had a lot of mileage on her. Soon an open Ferrari drew up and a small crowd collected. Our neighbour got into the car, while the crowd clapped and shouted 'Brigitte! Brigitte!'

I now had an interlude ashore until 1974 when I went to sea again, this time in a North Sea Survey boat as first mate. I did this for two years but found it pretty strenuous. North-west of Shetland in winter is just one gale after another. Nor was time in harbour, when we sheltered in Lerwick, much pleasanter. Two Christmases and New Years in the Shetlands, where the sun hardly bothers to rise in winter, was enough for me. If I felt really unhappy I would lie on my bunk thinking of all the lovely £10 notes I was earning, or playing imaginary games of golf round Liphook, but I was ready to hang up my sea boots in 1976.

It didn't really happen, of course. Someone asked me to take a 26-foot yacht from Paris to Lyons, which was great fun. Going through 140 locks in twelve days was hard work but the evenings made up for it. It was like motoring through a wine list – Sancerre, Pouilly, Nuits-St-George, Macon – we stopped at a different vineyard each night and did not fail to sample the local brew.

Nowadays the time passes very pleasantly. I have a one-day-a-week job which takes me to Lloyds in London. I spend much time making and painting signs for golf clubs, pubs and private houses, which brings in a little income. I go sailing in the Solent quite often in the season with a friend who has a 22-footer. But golf is my main occupation. It sounds like work but I sometimes play five times a week and love every minute of it. I even fool myself into thinking that I am getting better, but this can hardly be.

Writing these pages has brought back many happy, and some unhappy, memories. Fortunately the former well outweigh the latter. As it says on the sundial: *Horas non numero nisi serenas.*

NOTES

1. On 7 May 1915 RMS *Lusitania*, owned by the Cunard Line, was torpedoed by the German *U-20*, and sank in eighteen minutes, eleven miles off the Old Head of Kinsale, Ireland, killing 1,198 of the 1,959 people aboard.

2. On 10 October 1918 RMS *Leinster* was torpedoed by a German submarine not long after she had left Kingstown (Dun Laoghaire) harbour on her way to Holyhead. More than 500 passengers and crew lost their lives, including twenty-one post office staff who worked in the ship's sorting office and were attached to the Dublin Postal District.

3. A Very pistol fires flares, typically used for signalling at sea or from the ground to aircraft.

4. Lieutenant General Sir William Pike KCB CBE DSO: his son Lieutenant General Sir Hew Pike KCB DSO MBE commanded the Parachute Regiment in the Falklands War in 1982.

5. Marshal of the Royal Air Force Sir Thomas Geoffrey Pike GCB CBE DFC & Bar DL RAF (1906–83): he shot down four German aircraft.

6. Admiral of the Fleet David Beatty, 1st Earl Beatty, GCB OM GCVO DSO (1871–1936) commanded the British battlecruisers at the Battle of Jutland in 1916, when his aggressive approach was contrasted with the caution of his commander Admiral Jellicoe.

7. Admiral Sir John Frewen GCB (1911–75) served on Arctic convoys and as Squadron Navigating Officer for Aircraft Carriers in the Pacific 1939–45, and commanded HMS *Mounts Bay* in the Korean War. Later Flag Officer Second in Command at the Far East Station, Vice Chief of the Naval Staff, Commander-in-Chief, Home Fleet, Commander-in-Chief, Portsmouth and first Commander-in-Chief Naval Home Command. Also known from his appearance and his moods as 'Black Jack'.

8. Captain John H. Illingworth (1903–80), widely regarded as the founder of modern sailing.

9. Uppark or Up Park on the South Downs: now a National Trust property famous for its Grand Tour collection.

10. Norman Baillie-Stewart (1909–66). In 1933 he was court-martialled for selling military secrets to a foreign power and he was imprisoned in the Tower of London, the last Briton to be so. He took German citizenship in 1940 and became a propaganda broadcaster. Arrested in Austria in 1945 he was tried for assisting the enemy, pleaded guilty, and was sentenced to five years' imprisonment. On release he moved to Ireland under the pseudonym of James Scott, and died on a Dublin street of a heart attack in 1966.

11. Admiral John Casement CB (1877–1952): one of his brothers was called Roger (1864–1917) but was not the Irish nationalist Sir Roger Casement (1864–1916).

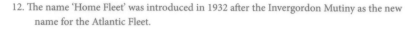

12. The name 'Home Fleet' was introduced in 1932 after the Invergordon Mutiny as the new name for the Atlantic Fleet.

13. Presumably Pamela Bird (1909–) only daughter of Sir Robert Bird, married 1st Reginald W. Bell (1934–46) and 2nd Alain de Mauduit, Vicomte de Kervern (1951–73) and 3rd changed her name by deed poll to Evans in 1974.

14. Major Sir Philip Hunloke (1865–1947), commodore of the Island Sailing Club 1901–03, Olympic yachtsman 1908, first President of the Ocean Racing Club, royal Sailing Master 1920–36, founder of the Fastnet Race 1925, commodore of the Royal Yacht Squadron from 1943 until his death in 1947 and one of the 20th century's greatest helmsmen.

15. Garfield 'Gar' Wood (1880–1971), an American inventor, entrepreneur, motorboat builder and racer who held the world water speed record on several occasions.

16. Lord Mountbatten was indeed blackballed twice by the Royal Yacht Squadron, and Queen Mary disapproved of Lady Mountbatten's behaviour, if only for the way she had danced the Charleston with Fred Astaire. King George V thought Mountbatten should be elected to the RYS, but there was a feeling amongst members that the candidate was a 'rackety young man with a weakness for showing off in fast motor boats'. Eventually Mountbatten was elected in 1943 by acclamation, and in 1957 he became a naval member of the RYS. He treated the episode as a joke.

17. The Ace of Spades, now only the name of a road junction, was in the 1930s a roadhouse, serving meals all day and night, with seating for 800, stage, dance music until the early hours, open-air swimming pool, miniature golf course, polo ground, riding school and an air strip.

18. But the Invergordon Mutiny took place in 1931 when then Commander Augustus Agar VC (1890–1968) was commanding the *Scarborough* in the West Indies. Later Captain Agar was a student on the Senior Officers' War Course at Greenwich, 1933–34.

19. Mount Bromo is an active volcano, over 7,000 ft, in eastern Java, which sits in a plain called the Sea of Sand.

20. The Dutch experimented from 1938 with a device called the snuiver, which worked as Wingfield describes, and which the Germans captured in 1940. He is mistaken that he saw this device before the war in the Far East.

21. Vice Admiral Sir David Gregory KBE CB DSO (1909–75) was Flag Officer, Scotland and Northern Ireland (1964–66). He commanded the submarines *Sturgeon* and *Traveller* and in September 1940 torpedoed a German troopship with the loss of 4,000 German soldiers.

22. The German *Admiral Graf Spee* was a pocket battleship, limited in tonnage by treaty but armed with six 280 mm (11 inch) guns and deployed as a commerce raider. She sank nine merchant ships, and several groups of British and French warships were diverted to hunting her down, before a heavy cruiser and two light cruisers of the Royal Navy and Royal New Zealand Navy chased her into Montevideo after the Battle of the River Plate on 13 December 1939.

23. The largest loss was three boats in two days: *Seahorse* and *Undine* on 7 January 1940, and *Starfish* on 9 January all off Heligoland. Then on 4 May 1940 *Seal* was captured in the Kattegat.

24. The Italian destroyer *Strale* rammed *Odin* just before midnight on 13 June 1940 and early next morning an Italian motor torpedo boat spotted the damaged *Odin* surfacing and finished her off by depth-charging her.

25. *The Naval Review*, 1949 number 3 pages 260–1, *Extra-Sensory Perception In Submarine Detection*, signed 'W'. The Editor invited comment and did indeed receive a pseudo-learned response.

26. Prime Minister Winston Churchill, 14 July 1940: 'Should the invader come to Britain, there will be no placid lying down of the people in submission before him, as we have seen, alas, in other countries. We shall defend every village, every town, and every city. The vast mass of London itself, fought street by street, could easily devour an entire hostile army; and we would rather see London laid in ruins and ashes than that it should be tamely and abjectly enslaved … London, if resolutely defended street by street, could swallow up an army …'.

27. HMS *Oxley* sunk off Obrestad, Norway by HMS *Triton* on 10 September 1939. Both boats had been in regular contact when *Triton* spotted an unidentified submarine which failed to reply to recognition signals flashed by *Triton*, and after several challenges she fired two torpedoes. *Triton* closed the sinking to find two survivors: Lieutenant Guy Watkins and Lieutenant Harry Stacey entered the water and rescued Lieutenant Commander H. G. Bowerman, *Oxley's* commanding officer and Able Seaman Guckes, a lookout. An inquiry found that *Oxley* was some way out of position and that *Triton* had acted correctly and was not culpable for the sinking.

28. Lieutenant R. E. Coltart in the submarine H49 sailed from Harwich on 17 October 1940 with orders to patrol off Texel and was lost later the same day.

29. Possibly a reference to Lieutenant P. J. Cowell, who sailed from Portsmouth in HMS *Swordfish* on 7 November 1940 and was not heard of until the wreck of his boat was found in 1983 a few miles south of St Catherine's Point, Isle of Wight with mine damage.

30. The obsolete French battleship *Paris* and several other French ships were seized in Portsmouth on 3 July 1940.

31. Lieutenant Commander David Wanklyn VC DSO (1911–42) was awarded the VC for his successful action against the 18,000 ton troopship *Conte Rosso* in May 1941, while surrounded by enemy destroyers. *Upholder* was destroyed by the Italian torpedo boat *Pegaso* off Tripoli on 14 April 1942.

32. Vice Admiral Sir Arthur Hezlet KBE CB DSO* DSC, a wartime submariner and later Flag Officer Submarines, wrote a comprehensive and definitive history, *British and Allied Submarine Operations in World War II* (Royal Navy Submarine Museum, 2001). In this and following chapters excerpts from Hezlet's record of events have been inserted as footnotes, to compare with Wingfield's personal and more detailed account.

33. Teddy Young (1913–2003) was the first RNVR officer to command a submarine and was awarded the DSO and DSC. His autobiographical *One of Our Submarines* (1952) with its distinctive cover, designed by Young, was the thousandth book published by Penguin.

34. HMS *Trinidad* sank on 15 May 1942.

35. Third Supplement to the *London Gazette*, 13 November 1942: for courage and skill in successful submarine patrols; to be companion of the Distinguished Service Order, Lieutenant-Commander Mervyn Robert George Wingfield, Royal Navy.

36. Wingfield has compounded two patrols. According to Hezlet: In early September *Sturgeon* was on a moving patrol line about 150 miles off Norway fjords from which German warships might emerge. On the first day Wingfield sighted a U-boat but too far off to attack, and later developed defects and had to return to base.

37. Operation Frankton: a raid on shipping in the German-occupied French port of Bordeaux, carried out by the Royal Marines Boom Patrol Detachment in December 1942. Twelve men in six canoes attacked shipping with Limpet mines: only two survived, their leader Major 'Blondie' Hasler and his crewman, Marine Bill Sparks. Six were executed by the Germans and two others were drowned. Mountbatten, chief of Combined Operations, called the raid 'the most courageous and imaginative of all the raids ever carried out by the men of Combined Operations'.

38. Operation Chariot: an amphibious attack on 28 March 1942 on the Normandie dry dock at St Nazaire in German-occupied France, by the Royal Navy and British commandos under Mountbatten's Combined Operations. The obsolete destroyer *Campbeltown*, packed with explosives, was rammed into the gates of the dry dock. Their small craft sunk, the commandos attempted to fight their way out of the town but were captured once they had run out of ammunition. Only 228 men returned to Britain, 169 were killed and 215 became prisoners of war. German casualties were over 360 dead, mostly killed while sightseeing on the *Campbeltown* when she blew up destroying the gates of the dock and preventing German heavy ships from using it. Five Victoria Crosses were awarded.

39. Commissioned as *P.339* and renamed *Taurus* at the end of 1942.

40. Admiral of the Fleet Sir Philip Vian GCB KBE DSO** (1894–1968), a controversial gunnery officer in both world wars, highly regarded as a fighting officer, but sometimes difficult and irascible. He commanded the destroyer *Cossack* during the *Altmark* incident, saw service in the Mediterranean in command of cruisers and aircraft carriers during the Allied invasions of Sicily and Italy, and at the end of World War II the aircraft carriers of the British Pacific Fleet.

41. Presumably Lieutenant Commander John Paton Fyfe DSC, who was commanding the submarine *Unruly* in 1942.

42. Captain George Barney Hamley Fawkes (1903–67), commanding officer, submarine depot ship *Maidstone* and captain, 8th Submarine Flotilla (Gibraltar, Algiers, Alexandria 1942–43), later Rear Admiral and Flag Officer Submarines.

43. Brickwoods: a Portsmouth brewery and Hampshire pub chain sold to Whitbread and closed in 1983. See pp. 45 & 92.

44. The Aletti hotel, now (2012) the Hotel Es Safir, and, despite its faded glory, one of the famous hotels of the world. In those days, Gibson wrote, 'the place for Services, the most expensive women (5,000 francs a night), and the hoarde of pressmen. At the long bar we usually met school friends, and recognised odd faces that we had not seen for

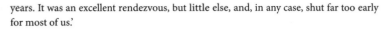

years. It was an excellent rendezvous, but little else, and, in any case, shut far too early for most of us.'

45. Oliver Baldwin, 2nd Earl Baldwin of Bewdley (1899–1958), son of the three times Prime Minster Stanley Baldwin, Eton and Guards, and a homosexual of changing political persuasions.

46. Lieutenant Commander Alastair Mars, DSO, DSC* (1915–85), was court-martialled and dismissed the service in 1952. He wrote several books including the autobiographical *Unbroken: The Story of a Submarine* (1953).

47. Supplement to the *London Gazette*, 19 October 1943: during this period Wingfield was awarded his first Distinguished Service Cross for outstanding bravery and skill in successful patrols in HM Submarines.

48. Tom Dunbabin DSO (1911–55) was a Tasmanian classical scholar and archaeologist, who joined the Special Operations Executive and directed Greek resistance forces on Crete. Presumably his kilt was Greek rather than Scots.

49. Henry 'Jumbo' Maitland Wilson, 1st Baron Wilson (1881–1964), who fought in the Boer War and World War I, was C.-in-C. Mediterranean in 1943 and Supreme Allied Commander Mediterranean in 1944.

50. Lieutenant John F. Gibson DSC RNVR, author of *Dark Seas Above* (1947): Gibson described the gun-layer, presumably Starbuck, as 'a great polar bear of a man, tough as granite, a great beard hiding his amused lips. He turned out to be our star performer, and to the very end, loved his gun as another man might love a dog or a pipe or a piece of land.'

51. Mitylene is the main town on the island of Lesbos.

52. Captain J. F. 'Jackie' Slaughter DSO RN (1905–80), captain of depot ship HMS *Cyclops* (1942–44) and captain of the depot ship HMS *Wolfe* and Captain, 2nd Submarine Flotilla (1944–45).

53. Captain 'Ginger' Cavenagh-Mainwaring (1908–2003): see obituary *Daily Telegraph* 5 April 2003.

54. *I-34* was carrying raw rubber bales, tungsten, tin, quinine, medicinal opium and samples of the Japanese weapons en route to German-occupied France and was due to pick up passengers at Penang.

55. Supplement to the *London Gazette*, 8 February 1944: for great courage, skill and undaunted devotion to duty in successful patrols in HM Submarines; bar to the Distinguished Service Cross, Lieutenant-Commander Mervyn Robert George Wingfield DSO DSC Royal Navy (Haslemere); the Distinguished Service Cross, Temporary Lieutenant (E) Anthony Ernest Corlett, Royal Navy (Newcastle); bar to the Distinguished Service Medal, Acting Chief Petty Officer Ernest Alfred Thomas, DSM, C/J.99723 (Eltham); Temporary Acting Leading Seaman Robert Tallis Hunt, C/SSX.2970I (Henley).

56. Supplement to the *London Gazette*, 19 October 1943: the Distinguished Service Medal for outstanding bravery and skill in successful patrols in HM Submarines to Petty Officer Steward Joseph John Knowles.

57. And an electronic search of the *London Gazette* has not revealed a reason either.

58. The officers of *U-852* were the only U-boat men to be convicted of war crimes. Heinz-Wilhelm Eck, his second-in-command August Hoffmann, and the ship's doctor Walter Weisspfennig were sentenced to death. Two others were imprisoned.

59. Eck's war diary was recovered and used in evidence against him.

60. Admiral of the Fleet Sir George Creasy GCB CBE DSO MVO (1895–1972), Director of Anti-Submarine Warfare in 1940–42 and Flag Officer Submarines in 1944–46.

61. Acting Captain Hugh Mundy DSC (1901–67) married Charlotte Elfreda 'Freda' Wingfield in 1923. He commanded HMS *Valluru*, the RN Air Station at Madras, 1944–45.

62. Admiral Charles Lockwood with Hans Christian Adamson, *Hellcats of the Sea* (Greenberg, New York, 1955).

63. Paul Hammond, New York property developer and salesman, and transatlantic yachtsman, who dined with King George V.

64. Rosa Lewis, née Ovenden (1867–1952), owner of the Cavendish Hotel at the corner of Jermyn and Duke Streets, London. Her friendships included Edward VII, with whom she was rumoured to have had an affair in the 1890s; Philippe, Comte de Paris; and Wilhelm II, whose portrait she hung in the men's lavatory. Rosa was known for her Robin Hood style whereby the rich paid for the poor and she continued this until her death.

65. Korvettenkapitän Adalbert Schnee (1913–82) commanded five U-boats and sank twenty-three ships (95,889 tons) and damaged three others (28,820 tons). Schnee held the Iron Cross 1st and 2nd classes, the Knight's Cross and the Knight's Cross with Oak Leaves. In September 1944 he took command of the U-2511, the first Type XXI boat to go on war patrol.

66. Vice Admiral Sir Peter Dawnay KCVO CB DSC LM (1904–89) married Lady Angela Christine Rose Montagu-Douglas-Scott, daughter of 7th Duke of Buccleuch.

67. Captain C. C. Hardy DSO* (1900–63), who though a 'spring bos'un' (specialist in physical training) had held several successful wartime commands including the escort *Falmouth*, the light cruiser *Cairo*, and the destroyer depot ship *Montclare*.

68. The Cunard liner RMS *Franconia* normally employed on the Liverpool–Halifax–Quebec route.

69. Admiral André Lemonnier (1896–1963), French Navy.

70. Admiral Sir William Geoffrey Arthur Robson KBE DSO* DSC (1902–89), Flag Officer Scotland 1953–56.

71. In the interwar years Teacher's Highland Cream was the leading Scotch whisky in North America: Ronald Teacher owned the Bermudan yawl *Mariella*.

72. Rear Admiral Sir Anthony 'Crap' Miers VC KBE CB DSO* (1906–85).

73. Admiral of the Fleet Sir Michael Le Fanu GCB DSC (1913–70)

INDEX